Lectures And Discourses - IV

by

Swami Vivekananda

Double9 BOOKS

Lectures And Discourses - IV

by Swami Vivekananda

ISBN: 978-93-59393-69-8

Published by

DOUBLE 9 BOOKS
2/13-B, Ansari Road
Daryaganj, New Delhi – 110002
info@double9books.com
www.double9books.com
Tel. 011-40042856

ABOUT THE AUTHOR

Swami Vivekananda was born Narendranath Datta in India on January 12, 1863. He died on July 4, 1902, and was the most important student of the Indian saint Ramakrishna. He was an important part of bringing Vedanta and Yoga to the West. He is also charged with making people more aware of other religions and making Hinduism a major world religion. Vivekananda had a lot of success at the Parliament. In the years that followed, he gave hundreds of lectures across the United States, England, and Europe to spread the main ideas of Hinduism. He also started the Vedanta Society of New York and the Vedanta Society of San Francisco, which is now the Vedanta Society of Northern California. Both of these groups became the basis for Vedanta Societies in the West. Vivekananda was one of the most important philosophers and social reformers in India at the time. He was also one of the most successful and powerful Vedanta missionaries in the West.People now think of him as one of the most important people in modern India and Hinduism. Mahatma Gandhi said that after reading Vivekananda's works, he loved his country a thousand times more.

CONTENTS

Discourses on Jnana-Yoga

I

(These were originally recorded by a prominent American disciple of the Swami, Miss S. E. Waldo. Swami Saradananda, while he was in America (1896), copied them out from her notebook — *Ed.*)

Om Tat Sat! To know the Om is to know the secret of the universe. The object of Jnâna-Yoga is the same as that of Bhakti and Râja Yogas, but the method is different. This is the Yoga for the strong, for those who are neither mystical nor devotional, but rational. As the Bhakti-Yogi works his way to complete oneness with the Supreme through love and devotion, so the Jnâna-Yogi forces his way to the realisation of God by the power of pure reason. He must be prepared to throw away all old idols, all old beliefs and superstitions, all desire for this world or another, and be determined only to find freedom. Without Jnana (knowledge) liberation cannot be ours. It consists in knowing what we really are, that we are beyond fear, beyond birth, beyond death. The highest good is the realisation of the Self. It is beyond sense, beyond thought. The *real* "I" cannot be grasped. It is the eternal subject and can never become the object of knowledge, because knowledge is only of the related, not of the Absolute. All sense-knowledge is limitation, it is an endless chain of cause and effect. This world is a relative world, a shadow of the real; still, being the plane of equipoise where happiness and misery are about evenly balanced, it is the only plane where man can realise his true Self and know that he is Brahman.

This world is "the evolution of nature and the manifestation of God". It is our interpretation of Brahman or the Absolute, seen through the veil of Mâyâ or appearance. The world is not zero, it has a certain reality; it only *appears* because Brahman *is*.

How shall we know the knower? The Vedanta says, "We are It, but can never know It, because It can never become the object of knowledge." Modern science also says that It cannot be known. We can, however, have glimpses of It from time to time. When the delusion of this world is once broken, it will come back to us, but no longer will it hold any reality for us. We shall know it as a mirage. To reach behind the mirage is the aim of all religions. That man and God are one is the constant teaching of the Vedas, but only few are able to penetrate behind the veil and reach the realisation of this truth.

The first thing to be got rid of by him who would be a Jnâni is fear. Fear is one of our worst enemies. Next, believe in nothing until you *know* it. Constantly tell yourself, "I am not the body, I am not the mind, I am not thought, I am not even consciousness; I am the Atman." When you can throw away *all*, only the true Self will remain. The Jnani's meditation is of two sorts: (1) to deny and think away everything we are *not*; (2) to insist upon what we really are — the Atman, the One Self — Existence, Knowledge, and Bliss. The true rationalist must go on and fearlessly follow his reason to its farthest limits. It will not answer to stop anywhere on the road. When we begin to deny, *all* must go until we reach what cannot be thrown away or denied, which is the real "I". That "I" is the witness of the universe, it is unchangeable, eternal, infinite. Now, layer after layer of ignorance covers it from our eyes, but it remains ever the same.

Two birds sat on one tree. The bird at the top was calm, majestic, beautiful, perfect. The lower bird was always hopping from twig to twig, now eating sweet fruits and being happy, now eating bitter fruits and being miserable. One day, when he had eaten a fruit more bitter than usual, he glanced up at the calm majestic upper bird and thought, "How I would like to be like him!" and he hopped up a little way towards him. Soon he forgot all about his desire to be like the upper bird, and went on as before, eating sweet and bitter fruits and being happy and miserable. Again he looked up, again he went up a little nearer to the calm and majestic upper bird. Many times was this repeated until at last he drew very near the upper bird; the brilliancy of his plumage dazzled him, seemed to absorb him, and finally, to his wonder and surprise, he found there was only one bird — he was the upper bird all the time and had but just found it out. Man is like that lower bird, but if he perseveres in his efforts to rise to the highest ideal he can conceive of, he too will find that he was the Self all the time and the other was but a dream. To separate ourselves utterly from matter and all belief in its reality is true Jnana. The Jnani must keep ever in his mind the "Om Tat Sat", that is, Om the only real existence. Abstract unity is the foundation of Jnana-Yoga. This is called Advaitism ("without dualism or dvaitism"). This is the corner-stone of the Vedanta philosophy, the Alpha and the Omega. "Brahman alone is true, all else is false and I am Brahman." Only by telling ourselves this until we make it a part of our very being, can we rise beyond all duality, beyond both good and evil, pleasure and pain, joy and sorrow, and know ourselves as the One, eternal, unchanging, infinite — the "One without a second".

The Jnana-Yogi must be as intense as the narrowest sectarian, yet as broad as the heavens. He must absolutely control his mind, be able to be a Buddhist or a Christian, to have the power to consciously divide himself into all these different ideas and yet hold fast to the eternal harmony. Constant drill alone can enable us to get this control. All variations are in the One, but we must learn not to identify ourselves with what we do, and to hear nothing, see nothing, talk of nothing but the thing in hand. We must put in our whole soul and be intense. Day and night tell yourself, "I am He, I am He."

II

(These were originally recorded by a prominent American disciple of the Swami, Miss S. E. Waldo. Swami Saradananda, while he was in America (1896), copied them out from her notebook — *Ed.*)

The greatest teacher of the Vedanta philosophy was Shankârachârya. By solid reasoning he extracted from the Vedas the truths of Vedanta, and on them built up the wonderful system of Jnâna that is taught in his commentaries. He unified all the conflicting descriptions of Brahman and showed that there is only one Infinite Reality. He showed too that as man can only travel slowly on the upward road, all the varied presentations are needed to suit his varying capacity. We find something akin to this in the teachings of Jesus, which he evidently adapted to the different abilities of his hearers. First he taught them of a Father in heaven and to pray to Him. Next he rose a step higher and told them, "I am the vine, you are the branches", and lastly he gave them the highest truth: "I and my Father are one", and "The Kingdom of Heaven is within you." Shankara taught that three things were the great gifts of God: (1) human body, (2) thirst after God, and (3) a teacher who can show us the light. When these three great gifts are ours, we may know that our redemption is at hand. Only knowledge can free and save us, but with knowledge must go virtue.

The essence of Vedanta is that there is but one Being and that every soul is that Being in full, not a part of that Being. *All* the sun is reflected in each dew-drop. Appearing in time, space and causality, this Being is man, as we know him, but behind all appearance is the one Reality. Unselfishness is the denial of the lower or apparent self. We have to free ourselves from this miserable dream that we are these bodies. We must *know* the truth, "I am He". We are not drops to fall into the ocean and be lost; each one is the *whole*, infinite ocean, and will know it when released from the fetters of illusion. Infinity cannot be divided, the "One without a second" can have no second, all *is* that One. This knowledge will come to all, but we should struggle to attain it now, because until we have it, we cannot really give mankind the best help. The Jivanmukta ('the living free' or one who knows) alone is able to give real love, real charity, real truth, and it is truth alone that makes us free. Desire makes slaves of us, it is an insatiable tyrant and gives its victims no rest; but the Jivanmukta has conquered all desire by rising to the knowledge that he is the One and there is nothing left to wish for.

The mind brings before us all our delusions — body, sex, creed, caste, bondage; so we have to tell the truth to the mind incessantly, until it is made to realise it. Our real nature is all bliss, and all the pleasure we know is but a reflection, an atom, of that bliss we get from touching our real nature. *That* is beyond both pleasure and pain. It is the "witness" of the universe, the unchanging reader before whom turn the leaves of the book of life.

Through practice comes Yoga, through Yoga comes knowledge, through knowledge love, and through love bliss.

"Me and mine" is a superstition; we have lived in it so long that it is well-nigh impossible to shake it off. Still we must get rid of it if we would rise to the highest. We must be bright and cheerful, long faces do not make religion. Religion should be the most joyful thing in the world, because it is the best. Asceticism cannot make us holy. Why should a man who loves God and who is pure be sorrowful? He should be like a happy child, be truly a child of God. The essential thing in religion is making the heart pure; the Kingdom of Heaven is within us, but only the pure in heart can see the King. While we think of the world, it is only the world for us; but let us come to it with the feeling that the world is God, and we shall have God. This should be our thought towards everyone and everything — parents, children, husbands, wives, friends, and enemies. Think how it would change the whole universe for us if we could consciously fill it with God! See nothing but God! All sorrow, all struggle, all pain would be for ever lost to us!

Jnana is "creedlessness", but that does not mean that it despises creeds. It only means that a stage above and beyond creeds has been gained. The Jnâni seeks not to destroy, but to help all. As all rivers roll their waters into the sea and become one, so all creeds should lead to Jnana and become one.

The reality of everything depends upon Brahman, and only as we really grasp this truth, have we any reality. When we cease to see any differences, then we know that "I and the Father are One".

Jnana is taught very clearly by Krishna in the Bhagavad-Gitâ. This great poem is held to be the Crown jewel of all Indian literature. It is a kind of commentary on the Vedas. It shows us that our battle for spirituality must be fought out in this life; so we must not flee from it, but rather compel it to give us all that it holds. As the Gita typifies this struggle for higher things, it is highly poetical to lay the scene in a battlefield. Krishna in the guise of a charioteer to Arjuna, leader of one of the opposing armies, urges him not to be sorrowful, not to fear death, since he knows he is immortal, that nothing which changes can be in the *real* nature of man. Through chapter after chapter, Krishna teaches the higher truths of philosophy and religion to Arjuna. It is these teachings which make this poem so wonderful; practically the whole of the Vedanta philosophy is included in them. The Vedas teach that the soul is infinite and in no way affected by the death of the body. The soul is a circle whose circumference is nowhere, but whose centre is in some body. Death (so-called) is but a change of centre. God is a circle whose circumference is nowhere and whose centre is everywhere, and when we can get out of the narrow centre of body, we shall realise God — our true Self.

The present is only a line of demarcation between the past and the future; so we cannot rationally say that we care only for the present, as it has no existence apart from the past and the future. It is all one complete whole, the idea of time being merely a condition imposed upon us by the form of our understanding.

III

(These were originally recorded by a prominent American disciple of the Swami, Miss S. E. Waldo. Swami Saradananda, while he was in America (1896), copied them out from her notebook — *Ed.*)

Jnâna teaches that the world should be given up, but not on that account to be abandoned. To be *in* the world, but not *of* it, is the true test of the Sannyâsin. This idea of renunciation has been in some form common to nearly all religions. Jnana demands that we look upon all alike, that we see only "sameness". Praise and blame, good and bad, even heat and cold, must be equally acceptable to us. In India there are many holy men of whom this is literally true. They wander on the snow-clad heights of the Himalayas or over the burning desert sands, entirely unclothed and apparently entirely unconscious of any difference in temperature.

We have first of all to give up this superstition of body; we are not the body. Next must go the further superstition that we are mind. We are not mind; it is but the "silken body", not any part of the soul. The mere word "body", applied to nearly all things, includes something common among all bodies. This is *existence*.

Our bodies are symbols of thought behind, and the thoughts themselves are in their turn symbols of something behind them, that is, the one Real Existence, the Soul of our soul, the Self of the universe, the Life of our life, our true Self. As long as we believe ourselves to be even the least different from God, fear remains with us; but when we know ourselves to be the One, fear goes: of what can we be afraid? By sheer force of will the Jnâni rises beyond body, beyond mind, making this universe zero. Thus he destroys Avidyâ and knows his true Self, the Âtman. Happiness and misery are only in the senses, they cannot touch our real Self. The soul is beyond time, space, and causality — therefore unlimited, omnipresent.

The Jnani has to come out of all forms, to get beyond all rules and books, and be his own book. Bound by forms, we crystallise and die. Still the Jnani must never condemn those who cannot yet rise above forms. He must never even think of another, "I am holier than thou".

These are the marks of the true Jnana-Yogi: (1) He desires nothing, save to know. (2) All his senses are under perfect restraint; he suffers everything without murmuring, equally content if his bed be the bare ground under the open sky, or if he is lodged in a king's palace. He shuns no suffering, he stands and bears it-he has given up all but the Self. (3) He knows that all but the One is unreal. (4) He has an intense desire for freedom. With a strong will, he fixes his mind on higher things and so attains to peace. If we know not peace, what are we more than the brutes? He does everything for others — for the Lord — giving up all fruits of work and looking for no result, either here or hereafter. What can the universe give us more than our own soul? Possessing that, we possess *all*. The Vedas teach that the Atman, or Self, is the One Undivided Existence. It is beyond mind, memory, thought, or even consciousness as we know it. From it are all things. It is that through which (or because of which) we see, hear, feel, and think. The goal of the universe is to realise oneness with the "Om" or One Existence. The Jnani has to be free from all forms; he is neither a Hindu, a Buddhist, nor a Christian, but he is all three. All action is renounced, given up to the Lord; then no action has power to bind. The Jnani is a tremendous rationalist; he denies everything. He tells himself day and night, "There are no beliefs, no sacred words, no heaven, no hell, no creed, no church — there is only Atman." When everything has been thrown away until what cannot be thrown away is reached, that is the Self. The Jnani takes nothing for granted; he analyses by pure reason and force of will, until he reaches Nirvâna which is the extinction of all relativity. No description or even conception of this state is possible. Jnana is never to be judged by any earthly result. Be not like the vulture which soars almost beyond sight, but which is ever ready to swoop downwards at the sight of a bit of carrion. Ask not for healing, or longevity, or prosperity, ask only to be free.

We are "Existence, Knowledge, Bliss" (Sachchidânanda). Existence is the last generalisation in the universe; so we exist, we know it; and bliss is the natural result of existence without alloy. Now and then we know a moment of supreme bliss, when we ask nothing, give nothing, and know nothing but bliss. Then it passes and we again see the panorama of the universe going on before us and we know it is but a "mosaic work set upon God, who is the background of all things". When we return to earth and see the Absolute as relative, we see Sachchidananda as Trinity — Father, Son, Holy Ghost. Sat = the creating principle; Chit = the guiding principle; Ânanda = the realising principle, which joins us again to the One. No one can know "existence" (Sat) except through "knowledge" (Chit), and hence the force of the saying of Jesus, No man can see the Father save through the Son. The Vedanta teaches that Nirvana can be attained here and now, that we do not have to wait for death to reach it. Nirvana is the realisation of the Self, and after having once, if only for an instant, known this, never again can one be deluded by the mirage of personality. Having eyes, we must see the apparent; but all the time we know it for what it is, we have found out its true nature. It is the "screen" that hides the Self which is unchanging. The screen opens and we find the Self behind it — all change is in the screen. In the saint the screen is thin and the Reality can almost shine through; but in the sinner it is thick, and we are apt to lose sight of the truth that the Atman is there, as well as behind the saint.

All reasoning ends only in finding Unity; so we first use analysis, then synthesis. In the world of science, the forces are gradually narrowed down in the search for one underlying force. When physical science can perfectly grasp the final unity, it will have reached an end, for reaching unity we find rest. Knowledge is final.

Religion, the most precious of all sciences, long ago discovered that final unity, to reach which is the object of Jnana-Yoga. There is but one Self in the universe, of which all lower selves are but manifestations. The Self, however, is infinitely more than all of its manifestations. All is the Self or Brahman. The saint, the sinner, the lamb, the tiger, even the murderer, as far as they have any reality, can be nothing else, because there is nothing else. "That which exists is One, sages call It variously." Nothing can be higher than this knowledge, and in those purified by Yoga it comes in flashes to the soul. The more one has been purified and prepared by Yoga and meditation, the clearer are these flashes of realisation. This was discovered 4,000 years ago, but has not yet become the property of the race; it is still the property of some individuals only.

IV

(These were originally recorded by a prominent American disciple of the Swami, Miss S. E. Waldo. Swami Saradananda, while he was in America (1896), copied them out from her notebook — *Ed.*)

All men, so-called, are not yet really human beings. Every one has to judge of this world through his own mind. The higher understanding is extremely difficult. The concrete is more to most people than the abstract. As an illustration of this, a story is told of two men in Bombay — one a Hindu and the other a Jain — who were playing chess in the house of a rich merchant of Bombay. The house was near the sea, the game long; the ebb and flow of the tide under the balcony where they sat attracted the attention of the players. One explained it by a legend that the gods in their play threw the water into a great pit and then threw it out again. The other said: No, the gods draw it up to the top of a high mountain to use it, and then when they have done with it, they throw it down again. A young student present began to laugh at them and said, "Do you not know that the attraction of the moon causes the tides?" At this, both men turned on him in a fury and inquired if he thought they were fools. Did he suppose that they believed the moon had any ropes to pull up the tides, or that it could reach so far? They utterly refused to accept any such foolish explanation. At this juncture the host entered the room and was appealed to by both parties. He was an educated man and of course knew the truth, but seeing plainly the impossibility of making the chess-players understand it, he made a sign to the student and then proceeded to give an explanation of the tides that proved eminently satisfactory to his ignorant hearers. "You must know", he told them, "that afar off in the middle of the ocean, there is a huge mountain of sponge — you have both seen sponge, and know what I mean. This mountain of sponge absorbs a great deal of the water and then the sea falls; by and by the gods come down and dance on the mountain and their weight squeezes all the water out and the sea rises again. This, gentlemen, is the cause of the tides, and you can easily see for yourselves how reasonable and simple is this explanation." The two men who ridiculed the power of the moon to cause the tides, found nothing incredible in a mountain of sponge, danced upon by the gods! The gods were real to them, and they had actually seen sponge; what was more likely than their joint effect upon the sea!

"Comfort" is no test of truth; on the contrary, truth is often far from being "comfortable". If one intends to really find truth, one must not cling to comfort. It is hard to let all go, but the Jnâni *must* do it. He must become pure, kill out all desires and cease to identify himself with the body. Then and then only, the higher truth can shine in his soul. Sacrifice is necessary, and this immolation of the lower self is the underlying truth that has made sacrifice a part of all religions. All the propitiatory offerings to the gods were but dimly understood types of the only sacrifice that is of any real value, the surrender of the apparent self, through which alone we can realise the higher Self, the Âtman. The Jnani must not try to preserve the body, nor even wish to do so. He must be strong and follow truth, though the universe fall. Those who follow "fads" can never do this. It is a life-work, nay, the work of a hundred lives! Only the few dare to realise the God within, to renounce heaven and Personal God and all hope of reward. A firm will is needed to do this; to be even vacillating is a sign of tremendous weakness. Man always is perfect, or he never could become so; but he had to realise it. If man were bound by external causes, he could only be mortal. Immortality can only be true of the unconditioned. Nothing can act on the Atman — the idea is pure delusion; but man must identify himself with that, not with body or mind. Let him know that he is the witness of the universe, then he can enjoy the beauty of the wonderful panorama passing before him. Let him even tell himself, "I am the universe, I am Brahman." When man *really* identifies himself with the One, the Atman, everything is possible to him and all matter becomes his servant. As Shri Ramakrishna has said: After the butter is churned, it can be put in water or milk and will never mix with either; so when man has once realised the Self, he can no more be contaminated by the world.

"From a balloon, no minor distinctions are visible, so when man rises high enough, he will not see good and evil people." "Once the pot is burned, no more can it be shaped; so with the mind that has once touched the Lord and has had a baptism of fire, no more can it be changed." Philosophy in Sanskrit means "clear vision", and religion is practical philosophy. Mere theoretic, speculative philosophy is not much regarded in India. There is no church, no creed, no dogma. The two great divisions are the "Dvaitists" and the "Advaitists". The former say, "The way to salvation is through the mercy of God; the law of causation, once set in motion, can never be broken; only God, who is not bound by this law, by His mercy helps us to break it". The latter say, "Behind all this nature is something that is free; and finding that which is beyond all law gets us freedom; and freedom is salvation." Dualism is only one phase, Advaitism goes to the ultimate. To become pure is the shortest path to freedom. Only that is ours which we earn. No authority can save us, no beliefs. If there is a God, *all* can find Him. No one needs to be told it is warm; each one can discover it for himself. So it should be with God. He should be a fact in the consciousness of all men. The Hindus do not recognise "sin", as it is understood by the Western mind. Evil deeds are not "sins", we are not offending some Ruler in committing these; we are simply injuring ourselves, and we must suffer the penalty. It is not a sin to put one's finger in the fire, but he who does so will surely suffer just as much as if it were. All deeds produce certain results, and "every deed returns to the doer". "Trinitarianism" is an advance on "Unitarianism" (which is dualism, God and man for ever separate). The first step upwards is when we recognise ourselves as the children of God; the last step is when we realise ourselves as the One, the Atman.

V

(These were originally recorded by a prominent American disciple of the Swami, Miss S. E. Waldo. Swami Saradananda, while he was in America (1896), copied them out from her notebook — *Ed.*)

The question why there cannot be eternal bodies is in itself illogical, as "body" is a term applied to a certain combination of elements, changeable and in its very nature impermanent. When we are not passing through changes, we will not have bodies (so-called). "Matter" beyond the limit of time, space, and causality will not be matter at all. Time and space exist only in us, we are the one Permanent Being. All forms are transitory, that is why all religions say, "God has no form". Menander was a Greco-Bactrian king. He was converted to Buddhism about 150 B.C. by one of the Buddhist missionary monks and was called by them "Milinda". He asked a young monk, his teacher, "Can a perfect man (such as Buddha) be in error or make mistakes?" The young monk's answer was : The perfect man can remain in ignorance of minor matters not in his experience, but he can *never* be in error as to what his insight has actually realised. He is perfect here and now. He knows the whole mystery, the Essence of the universe, but he may not know the mere external variation through which that Essence is manifested in time and space. He knows the *clay* itself, but has not had experience of every shape it may be wrought into. The perfect man knows the Soul itself, but not every form and combination of its manifestation. He would have to attain more relative knowledge just as we do, though on account of his immense power, he would learn it far more quickly.

The tremendous "search-light" of a perfectly controlled mind, when thrown on any subject, would rapidly reduce it to possession. It is very important to understand this, because it saves so much foolish explanation as to how a Buddha or a Jesus could be mistaken in ordinary relative Knowledge, as we well know they were. The disciples should not be blamed as having put down the sayings erroneously. It is humbug to say that one thing is true and another untrue in their statements. Accept the whole account, or reject it. How can *we* pick out the true from the false?

If a thing happens once, it can happen again. If any human being has ever realised perfection, we too can do so. If we cannot become perfect here and now, we never can in any state or heaven or condition we may imagine. If Jesus Christ was not perfect, then the religion bearing his name falls to the ground. If he was perfect, then we too can become perfect. The perfect man does not reason or "know", as we count "knowing", for all our knowledge is mere comparison, and there is no comparison, no classification, possible in the Absolute. Instinct is less liable to error than reason, but reason is higher and leads to intuition, which is higher still. Knowledge is the parent of intuition, which like instinct, is also unerring, but on a higher plane. There are three grades of manifestation in living beings: (1) sub-conscious — mechanical, unerring; (2) conscious — knowing, erring; (3) superconscious — intuitional, unerring; and these are illustrated in an animal, man, and God. For the man who has become perfect, nothing remains but to apply his understanding. He lives only to help the world, desiring nothing for himself. What distinguishes is negative — the positive is ever wider and wider. What we have in common is the widest of all, and that is "Being".

"Law is a mental shorthand to explain a series of phenomena"; but law as an entity, so to speak, does not exist. We use the word to express the regular succession of certain occurrences in the phenomenal world. We must not let law become a superstition, a something inevitable, to which we must submit. Error must accompany reason, but the very struggle to conquer error makes us gods. Disease is the struggle of nature to cast out something wrong; so sin is the struggle of the divine in us to throw off the animal. We must "sin" (that is, make mistakes) in order to rise to Godhood.

Do not pity anyone. Look upon all as your equal, cleanse yourself of the primal sin of inequality. We are all equal and must not think, "I am good and you are bad, and I am trying to reclaim you". Equality is the sign of the free. Jesus came to publicans and sinners and lived with them. He never set himself on a pedestal. Only sinners see sin. See not man, see only the Lord. We manufacture our own heaven and can make a heaven even in hell. Sinners are only to be found in hell, and as long as we see them around us, we are there ourselves. Spirit is not in time, nor in space. Realise "I am Existence Absolute, Knowledge Absolute, Bliss Absolute — I am He, I am He". Be glad at birth, be glad at death, rejoice always in the love of God. Get rid of the bondage of body; we have become slaves to it and learnt to hug our chains and love our slavery; so much so that we long to perpetuate it, and go on with "body" "body" for ever. Do not cling to the idea of "body", do not look for a future existence in any way like this one; do not love or want the body, even of those dear to us. This life is our teacher, and dying only makes room to begin over again. Body is our schoolmaster, but to commit suicide is folly, it is only killing the "schoolmaster". Another will take his place. So until we have learnt to transcend the body, we must have it, and losing one, will get another. Still we must not identify ourselves with the body, but look upon it only as an instrument to be used in reaching perfection. Hanumân, the devotee of Râma, summed up his philosophy in these words: When I identify myself with the body, O Lord, I am Thy creature, eternally separate from Thee. When I identify myself with the soul, I am a spark of that Divine Fire which Thou art. But when I identify myself with the Atman, I and Thou art one.

Therefore the Jnani strives to realise the Self and nothing else.

VI

(These were originally recorded by a prominent American disciple of the Swami, Miss S. E. Waldo. Swami Saradananda, while he was in America (1896), copied them out from her notebook — *Ed.*)

Thought is all important, for "what we think we become". There was once a Sannyâsin, a holy man, who sat under a tree and taught the people. He drank milk, and ate only fruit, and made endless "Prânâyâmas", and felt himself to be very holy. In the same village lived an evil woman. Every day the Sannyasin went and warned her that her wickedness would lead her to hell. The poor woman, unable to change her method of life which was her only means of livelihood, was still much moved by the terrible future depicted by the Sannyasin. She wept and prayed to the Lord, begging Him to forgive her because she could not help herself. By and by both the holy man and the evil woman died. The angels came and bore her to heaven, while the demons claimed the soul of the Sannyasin. "Why is this!" he exclaimed, "have I not lived a most holy life, and preached holiness to everybody? Why should I be taken to hell while this wicked woman is taken to heaven?" "Because," answered the demons, "while she was forced to commit unholy acts, her mind was always fixed on the Lord and she sought deliverance, which has now come to her. But you, on the contrary, while you performed only holy acts, had your mind always fixed on the wickedness of others. You saw only sin, and thought only of sin, so now you have to go to that place where only sin is." The moral of the story is obvious: The outer life avails little. The heart must be pure and the pure heart sees only good, never evil. We should never try to be guardians of mankind, or to stand on a pedestal as saints reforming sinners. Let us rather purify ourselves, and the result must be that in so doing we shall help others.

Physics is bounded on both sides by metaphysics. So it is with reason — it starts from non-reason and ends with non-reason. If we push inquiry far enough in the world of perception, we must reach a plane beyond perception. Reason is really stored up and classified perception, preserved by memory. We can never imagine or reason beyond our sense-perceptions. Nothing beyond reason can be an object of sense-knowledge. We feel the limited character of reason, yet it does bring us to a plane where we get a glimpse of something beyond. The question then arises: Has man an instrument that transcends reason? It is very probable that in man there is a power to reach beyond reason; in fact the saints in all ages assert the existence of this power in themselves. But it is impossible in the very nature of things to translate spiritual ideas and perceptions into the language of reason; and these saints, each and all, have declared their inability to make known their spiritual experiences. Language can, of course, supply no words for them, so that it can only be asserted that these are actual experiences and can be had by all. Only in that way can they become known, but they can never be described. Religion is the science which learns the transcendental in nature through the transcendental in man. We know as yet but little of man, consequently but little of the universe. When we know more of man, we shall probably know more of the universe. Man is the epitome of all things and all knowledge is in him. Only for the infinitesimal portion of the universe, which comes into sense-perception, are we able to find a reason; never can we give the reason for any fundamental principle. Giving a reason for a thing is simply to classify it and put it in a pigeon-hole of the mind. When we meet a new fact, we at once strive to put it in some existing category and the attempt to do this is to reason. When we succeed in placing the fact, it gives a certain amount of satisfaction, but we can never go beyond the physical plane in this classification. That man can transcend the limits of the senses is the emphatic testimony of all past ages. The Upanishads told 5,000 years ago that the realisation of God could never be had through the senses. So far, modern agnosticism agrees, but the Vedas go further than the negative side and assert in the plainest terms that man can and does transcend this sense-bound, frozen universe. He can, as it were, find a hole in the ice, through which he can pass and reach the whole ocean of life. Only by so transcending the world of sense, can he reach his true Self and realise what he really is.

Jnâna is never sense-knowledge. We cannot *know* Brahman, but we *are* Brahman, the whole of It, not a piece. The unextended can never be divided. The apparent variety is but the reflection seen in time and space, as we see the sun reflected in a million dewdrops, though we know that the sun itself is one and not many. In Jnana we have to lose sight of the variety and see only the Unity. Here there is no subject, no object, no knowing, no thou or he or I, only the one, absolute Unity. We *are* this all the time; once free, ever free. Man is *not* bound by the law of causation. Pain and misery are not in man, they are but as the passing cloud throwing its shadow over the sun, but the cloud passes, the sun is unchanged; and so it is with man. He is not born, he does not die, he is not in time and space. These ideas are mere reflections of the mind, but we mistake them for the reality and so lose sight of the glorious truth they obscure. Time is but the method of our thinking, but we are the eternally present tense. Good and evil have existence only in relation to us. One cannot be had without the other, because neither has meaning or existence apart from the other. As long as we recognise duality, or separate God and man, so long we must see good and evil. Only by going to the centre, by unifying ourselves with God can we escape the delusions of the senses. When we let go the eternal fever of desire, the endless thirst that gives us no rest, when we have for ever quenched desire, we shall escape both good and evil, because we shall have transcended both. The satisfaction of desire only increases it, as oil poured on fire but makes it burn more fiercely. The further from the centre, the faster goes the wheel, the less the rest. Draw near the centre, check desire, stamp it out, let the false self go, then our vision will clear and we shall see God. Only through renunciation of this life and of all life to come (heaven etc.), can we reach the point where we stand firmly on the true Self. While we hope for anything, desire still rules us. Be for one moment really "hopeless", and the mist will clear. For what to hope when one is the all of existence? The secret of Jnana is to give up all and be sufficient unto ourselves. Say "not", and you become "not"; say "is", and you become "is". Worship the Self within, naught else exists. All that binds us is Mâyâ-delusion.

VII

(These were originally recorded by a prominent American disciple of the Swami, Miss S. E. Waldo. Swami Saradananda, while he was in America (1896), copied them out from her notebook — *Ed.*)

The Self is the condition of all in the universe, but It can never be conditioned. As soon as we know that we are It, we are free. As mortals we are not and never can be free. Free mortality is a contradiction in terms, for mortality implies change, and only the changeless can be free. The Atman alone is free, and that is our real essence. We feel this inner freedom; in spite of all theories, all beliefs, we know it, and every action proves that we know it. The will is not free, its apparent freedom is but a reflection from the Real. If the world were only an endless chain of cause and effect, where could one stand to help it? There must needs be a piece of dry land for the rescuer to stand on, else how can he drag anyone out of the rushing stream and save him from drowning? Even the fanatic who cries "I am a worm", thinks that he is on the way to become a saint. He sees the saint even in the worm.

There are two ends or aims of human life, real knowing (Vijnâna) and bliss. Without freedom, these two are impossible. They are the touchstone of all life. We should feel the Eternal Unity so much, that we should weep for all sinners, knowing that it is we who are sinning. The eternal law is self-sacrifice, not self-assertion. What self to assert when all is one? There are no "rights", all is love. The great truths that Jesus taught have never been lived. Let us try his method and see if the world will not be saved. The contrary method has nearly destroyed it. Selflessness only, not selfishness, can solve the question. The idea of "right" is a limitation; there is really no "mine" and "thine", for I am thou and thou art I. We have "responsibility", not "rights". We should say, "I am the universe", not "I am John" or "I am Mary". These limitations are all delusions and are what holds us in bondage, for as soon as I think, "I am John", I want exclusive possession of certain things and begin to say "me and mine", and continually make new distinctions in so doing. So our bondage goes on increasing with every fresh distinction, and we get further and further away from the central Unity, the undivided Infinite. There is only one Individual, and each of us is That. Oneness alone is love and fearlessness; separation leads us to hatred and fear. Oneness fulfils the law. Here, on earth, we strive to enclose little spaces and exclude outsiders, but we cannot do that in the sky, though that is what sectarian religion tries to do when it says, "Only *this* way leads to salvation, all others are wrong". Our aim should be to wipe out these little enclosures to widen the boundaries until they are lost sight of, and to realise that all religions lead to God. This little puny self must be sacrificed. This is the truth symbolised by baptism into a new life, the death of the old man, the birth of the new — the perishing of the false self, the realisation of the Atman, the one Self of the universe.

The two great divisions of the Vedas are Karma Kânda — the portion pertaining to doing or work, and Jnâna Kânda — the portion treating of knowing, true knowledge. In the Vedas we can find the whole process of the growth of religious ideas. This is because when a higher truth was reached, the lower perception that led to it, was still preserved. This was done, because the sages realised that the world of creation being eternal, there would always be those who needed the first steps to knowledge, that the highest philosophy, while open to all, could never be grasped by all. In nearly every other religion, only the last or highest realisation of truth has been preserved, with the natural consequence that the older ideas were lost, while the newer ones were only understood by the few and gradually came to have no meaning for the many. We see this result illustrated in the growing revolt against old traditions and authorities. Instead of accepting them, the man of today boldly challenges them to give reasons for their claims, to make clear the grounds upon which they demand acceptance. Much in Christianity is the mere application of new names and meanings to old pagan beliefs and customs. If the old sources had been preserved and the reasons for the transitions fully explained, many things would have been clearer. The Vedas preserved the old ideas and this fact necessitated huge commentaries to explain them and why they were kept. It also led to many superstitions, through clinging to old forms after all sense of their meaning had been lost. In many ceremonials, words are repeated which have survived from a now forgotten language and to which no real meaning can now be attached. The idea of evolution was to be found in the Vedas long before the Christian era; but until Darwin said it was true, it was regarded as a mere Hindu superstition.

All external forms of prayer and worship are included in the Karma Kanda. These are good when performed in a spirit of unselfishness and not allowed to degenerate into mere formality. They purify the heart. The Karma-Yogi wants everyone to be saved before himself. His only salvation is to help others to salvation. "To serve Krishna's servants is the highest worship." One great saint prayed, "Let me go to hell with the sins of the whole world, but let the world be saved." This true worship leads to intense self-sacrifice. It is told of one sage that he was willing to give all his virtues to his dog, that it might go to heaven, because it had long been faithful to him, while he himself was content to go to hell.

The Jnana Kanda teaches that knowledge alone can save, in other words, that he must become "wise unto salvation". Knowledge is first objective, the Knower knowing Himself. The Self, the only subject, is in manifestation seeking only to know Itself. The better the mirror, the better reflection it can give; so man is the best mirror, and the purer the man, the more clearly he can reflect God. Man makes the mistake of separating himself from God and identifying himself with the body. This mistake arises through Maya, which is not exactly delusion but might be said to be seeing the real as something else and not as it is. This identifying of ourselves with the body leads to inequality, which inevitably leads to struggle and jealousy, and so long as we see inequality, we can never know happiness. "Ignorance and inequality are the two sources of all misery", says Jnana.

When man has been sufficiently buffeted by the world, he awakes to a desire for freedom; and searching for means of escape from the dreary round of earthly existence, he seeks knowledge, learns what he really is, and is free. After that he looks at the world as a huge machine, but takes good care to keep his fingers out of the wheels. Duty ceases for him who is free; what power can constrain the free being? He does good, because it is his nature, not because any fancied duty commands it. This does not apply to those who are still in the bondage of the senses. Only for him, who has transcended the lower self, is this freedom. He stands on his own soul, obeys no law; he is free and perfect. He has undone the old superstitions and got out of the wheel. Nature is but the mirror of our own selves. There is a limit to the working power of human beings, but no limit to desire; so we strive to get hold of the working powers of others and enjoy the fruits of their labours, escaping work ourselves. Inventing machinery to work for us can never increase well-being, for in gratifying desire, we only find it, and then we want more and more without end. Dying, still filled with ungratified desires, we have to be born again and again in the vain search for satisfaction. "Eight Millions of bodies have we had, before we reached the human", say the Hindus. Jnana says, "Kill desire and so get rid of it". That is the only way. Cast out all causation and realise the Atman. Only freedom can produce true morality. If there were only an endless chain of cause and effect, Nirvâna could not be. It is extinction of the seeming self, bound by this chain. That is what constitutes freedom, to get beyond causality.

Our true nature is good, it is free, the pure being that can never be or do wrong. When we read God with our eyes and minds, we call Him this or that; but in reality there is but One, all variations are our interpretations of that One. We *become* nothing; we *regain* our true Self. Buddha's summary of misery as the outcome of "ignorance and caste" (inequality) has been adopted by the Vedantists, because it is the best ever made. It manifests the wonderful insight of this greatest among men. Let us then be brave and sincere: whatever path we follow with devotion, must take us to freedom. Once lay hold of one link of the chain and the whole must come after it by degrees. Water the root of the tree and the whole tree is watered. It is of little advantage to waste time to water each leaf. In other words, seek the Lord and getting Him we get all. Churches, doctrines, forms — these are merely the hedges to protect the tender plant of religion; but later on they must all be broken down, that the little plant may become a tree. So the various religious sects, Bibles, Vedas, and scriptures are just "tubs" for the little plant; but it has to get out of the tub and fill the world.

We must learn to feel ourselves as much in the sun, in the stars, as here. Spirit is beyond all time and space; every eye seeing is my eye; every mouth praising the Lord is my mouth; every sinner is I. We are confined nowhere, we are not body. The universe is our body. We are just the pure crystal reflecting all, but itself ever the same. We are magicians waving magic wands and creating scenes before us at will, but we have to go behind appearances and know the Self. This world is like water in a kettle, beginning to boil; first a bubble comes, then another, then many until all is in ebullition and passes away in steam. The great teachers are like the bubbles as they begin — here one, there one; but in the end every creature has to be a bubble and escape. Creation, ever new, will bring new water and go through the process all over again. Buddha and Christ are the two greatest "bubbles" the world has known. They were great souls who having realised freedom helped others to escape. Neither was perfect, but they are to be judged by their virtues, never by their defects. Jesus fell short, because he did not always live up to his own highest ideal; and above all, because he did not give woman an equal place with man. Woman did everything for him, yet not one was made an apostle. This was doubtless owing to his Semitic origin. The great Aryans, Buddha among the rest, have always put woman in an equal position with man. For them sex in religion did not exist. In the Vedas and Upanishads, women taught the highest truths and received the same veneration as men.

VIII

(These were originally recorded by a prominent American disciple of the Swami, Miss S. E. Waldo. Swami Saradananda, while he was in America (1896), copied them out from her notebook — *Ed.*)

Both happiness and misery are chains, the one golden, the other iron; but both are equally strong to bind us and hold us back from realising our true nature. The Atman knows neither happiness nor misery. These are mere "states", and states must ever change. The nature of the soul is bliss and peace unchanging. We have not to *get* it; we *have* it; let us wash away the dross from our eyes and see it. We must stand ever on the Self and look with perfect calmness upon all the panorama of the world. It is but baby's play and ought never to disturb us. If the mind is pleased by praise, it will be pained by blame. All pleasures of the senses or even of the mind are evanescent, but within ourselves is the one true unrelated pleasure, dependent on nothing outside. "The pleasure of the Self is what the world calls religion." The more our bliss is within, the more spiritual we are. Let us not depend upon the world for pleasure.

Some poor fishwives, overtaken by a violent storm, found refuge in the garden of a rich man. He received them kindly, fed them, and left them to rest in a summer-house, surrounded by exquisite flowers which filled all the air with their rich perfume. The women lay down in this sweet-smelling paradise, but could not sleep. They missed something out of their lives and could not be happy without it. At last one of the women arose and went to the place where they had left their fish baskets, brought them to the summer-house, and then once more happy in the familiar smell, they were all soon sound asleep.

Let not the world be our "fish basket" which we have to depend upon for enjoyment. This is Tâmasika, or being bound by the lowest of the three qualities (or Gunas). Next higher come the egotistical who talk always about "I", "I". Sometimes they do good work and may become spiritual. These are Râjasika or active. Highest come the introspective nature (Sâttvika), those who live only in the Self. These three qualities are in every human being in varying proportions, and different ones predominate at different times. We must strive to overcome Tamas with Rajas and then to submerge both in Sattva.

Creation is not a "making" of something, it is the struggle to regain equilibrium, as when atoms of cork are thrown to the bottom of a pail of water: they rush to the top singly and in clusters, and when all have reached the top and equilibrium has been regained, all motion or "life" ceases. So with creation; if equilibrium were reached, all change would cease and life, so-called, would end. Life must be accompanied with evil, for when the balance is regained, the world must end, as sameness and destruction are one. There is no possibility of ever having pleasure without pain, or good without evil, for living itself is just the lost equilibrium. What we want is freedom, not life, nor pleasure, nor good. Creation is eternal, without beginning, without end, the ever moving ripple in an infinite lake. There are yet unreached depths and others where stillness has been regained, but the ripple is ever progressing, the struggle to regain the balance is eternal. Life and death are but different names for the same fact, they are the two sides of one coin. Both are Mâyâ, the inexplicable state of striving at one point to live and a moment later to die. Beyond all this is the true nature, the Atman. We enter into creation, and then, for us, it becomes living. Things are dead in themselves, only we give them life, and then, like fools, we turn round and are afraid of them or enjoy them! The world is neither true nor untrue, it is the shadow of truth.

"Imagination is the gilded shadow of truth", says the poet. The internal universe, the Real, is infinitely greater than the external one, which is but the shadowy projection of the true one. When we see the "rope", we do not see the "serpent", and when the "serpent" is, the "rope" is not. Both cannot exist at the same time; so while we see the world we do not realise the Self, it is only an intellectual concept. In the realisation of Brahman, the personal "I" and all sense of the world is lost. The Light does not know the darkness, because it has no existence in the light; so Brahman is all. While we recognise a God, it is really only the Self that we have separated from ourselves and worship as outside of us; but all the time it is our own true Self, the one and only God. The nature of the brute is to remain where he is, of man to seek good and avoid evil, of God to neither seek nor avoid, but just to be blissful eternally. Let us be Gods, let us make our hearts like an ocean, to go beyond all the trifles of the world and see it only as a picture. We can then enjoy it without being in any way affected by it. Why look for good in the world, what can we find there? The best it has to offer is only as if children playing in a mud puddle found a few glass beads. They lose them again and have to begin the search anew. Infinite strength is religion and God. We are only souls if we are free, there is immortality only if we are free, there is God only if He is free.

Until we give up the world manufactured by the ego, never can we enter the Kingdom of Heaven. None ever did, none ever will. To give up the world is to utterly forget the ego, to know it not at all, living in the body but not being ruled by it. This rascal ego must be obliterated. Power to help mankind is with the silent ones who only live and love and withdraw their own personality entirely. They never say "me" or "mine", they are only blessed in being the instruments to help others. They are wholly identified with God, asking nothing and not *consciously* doing anything. They are the true Jivanmuktas — the absolutely selfless, their little personality thoroughly blown away, ambition non-existent. They are all principle, with no personality. The more we sink the "little self", the more God comes. Let us get rid of the little "I" and let only the great "I" live in us. Our best work and our greatest influence is when we are without a thought of self. It is the "desireless" who bring great results to pass. Bless men when they revile you. Think how much good they are doing by helping to stamp out the false ego. Hold fast to the real Self, think only pure thoughts, and you will accomplish more than a regiment of mere preachers. Out of purity and silence comes the word of power.

IX

(These were originally recorded by a prominent American disciple of the Swami, Miss S. E. Waldo. Swami Saradananda, while he was in America (1896), copied them out from her notebook — *Ed.*)

Expression is necessarily degeneration, because spirit can only be expressed by the "letter", and as St. Paul said, "the letter killeth". Life cannot be in the "letter" which is only a reflection. Yet, principle must be clothed in matter to be "known". We lose sight of the Real in the covering and come to consider that as the Real, instead of as the symbol. This is an almost universal mistake. Every great Teacher knows this and tries to guard against it; but humanity, in general, is prone to worship the *seen* rather than the unseen. This is why a succession of prophets have come to the world to point again and again to the principle behind the personality and to give it a new covering suited to the times. Truth remains ever unchanged, but it can only be presented in a "form"; so from time to time a new "form" or expression is given to Truth, as the progress of mankind makes them ready to receive it. When we free ourselves from name and form, especially when we no longer need a body of any kind, good or bad, coarse or fine, then only do we escape from bondage. "Eternal progression" would be eternal bondage. We must get beyond all differentiation and reach eternal "sameness" or homogeneity or Brahman. The Atman is the unity of all personalities and is unchangeable, the "One without a second". It is not life, but it is coined into life. It is beyond life and death and good and bad. It is the Absolute Unity. Dare to seek Truth even through hell. Freedom can never be true of name and form, of the related. No form can say, "I am free as a form." Not until all idea of form is lost, does freedom come. If our freedom hurts others, we are not free there. We must not hurt others. While real perception is only one, relative perceptions must be many. The fountain of all knowledge is in every one of us — in the ant as in the highest angel. Real religion is one; all quarrel is with the forms, the symbols, the "illustrations". The millennium exists already for those who find it. The truth is, we have lost ourselves and think the world to be lost. "Fool! Hearest not thou? In thine own heart, day and night, is singing that Eternal Music — Sachchidânanda, Soham, Soham, (Existence, Knowledge, and Bliss, I am He, I am He)!"

To try to think without a phantasm is to try to make the impossible possible. Each thought has two parts — the thinking and the word, and we must have both. Neither idealists nor materialists are able to explain the world; to do that, we must take both idea and expression. All knowledge is of the reflected as we can only see our own faces reflected in a mirror. So no one can know his Self or Brahman; but each is that Self and must see it reflected in order to make it an object of knowledge. This seeing the illustrations of the unseen Principle is what leads to idolatry — so-called. The range of idols is wider than is usually supposed. They range from wood and stone to great personalities as Jesus or Buddha. The introduction of idols into India was the result of Buddha's constantly inveighing against a Personal God. The Vedas knew them not, but the reaction against the loss of God as Creator and Friend led to making idols of the great teachers, and Buddha himself became an idol and is worshipped as such by millions of people. Violent attempts at reform always end in retarding true reform. To worship is inherent in every man's nature; only the highest philosophy can rise to pure abstraction. So man will ever personify his God in order to worship Him. This is very good, as long as the symbol, be it what it may, is worshipped as a symbol of the Divinity behind and not in and for itself. Above all, we need to free ourselves from the superstition of believing because "it is in the books". To try to make everything — science, religion, philosophy, and all — conform to what any book says, is a most horrible tyranny. Book-worship is the worst form of idolatry. There was once a stag, proud and free, and he talked in a lordly fashion to his child, "Look at me, see my powerful horns! With one thrust I can kill a man; it is a fine thing to be a stag!" Just then the sound of the huntsman's bugle was heard in the distance, and the stag precipitately fled, followed by his wondering child.

When they had reached a place of safety, he inquired, "Why do you fly before man, O my father, when you are so strong and brave?" The stag answered, "My child, I know I am strong and powerful, but when I hear that sound, something seizes me and makes me fly whether I will or no." So with us. We hear the "bugle sound" of the laws laid down in the books, habits and old superstitions lay hold of us; and before we know it, we are fast bound and forget our real nature which is freedom.

Knowledge exists eternally. The man who discovers a spiritual truth is what we call "inspired", and what he brings to the world is revelation. But revelation too is eternal and is not to be crystallised as final and then blindly followed. Revelation may come to any man who has fitted himself to receive it. Perfect purity is the most essential thing, for only "the pure in heart shall see God". Man is the highest being that exists and this is the greatest world, for here can man realise freedom. The highest concept we can have of God is man. Every attribute we give Him belongs also to man, only in a lesser degree. When we rise higher and want to get out of this concept of God, we have to get out of the body, out of mind and imagination, and leave this world out of sight. When we rise to be the absolute, we are no longer in the world — all is Subject, without object. Man is the apex of the only "world" we can ever know. Those who have attained "sameness" or perfection, are said to be "living in God". All hatred is "killing the self by the self"; therefore, love is the law of life. To rise to this is to be perfect; but the more "perfect" we are, the less work can we do. The Sattvika see and know that all this world is mere child's play and do not trouble themselves about that. We are not much disturbed when we see two puppies fighting and biting each other. We know it is not a serious matter. The perfect one knows that this world is Mâyâ. Life is called Samsâra — it is the result of the conflicting forces acting upon us. Materialism says, "The voice of freedom is a delusion." Idealism says, "The voice that tells of bondage is but a dream." Vedanta says, "We are free and not free at the same time." That means that we are never free on the earthly plane, but ever free on the spiritual side. The Self is beyond both freedom and bondage. We *are* Brahman, we *are* immortal knowledge beyond the senses, we *are* Bliss Absolute.

Six Lessons On Raja-Yoga

(These lessons are composed of notes of class talks given by Swami Vivekananda to an intimate audience in the house of Mrs. Sara C. Bull, a devoted American disciple, and were preserved by her and finally printed in 1913 for private circulation — *Ed.*)

Râja-Yoga is as much a science as any in the world. It is an analysis of the mind, a gathering of the facts of the supersensuous world and so building up the spiritual world. All the great spiritual teachers the world has known said, "I see and I know." Jesus, Paul, and Peter all claimed actual perception of the spiritual truths they taught.

This perception is obtained by Yoga.

Neither memory nor consciousness can be the limitation of existence. There is a superconscious state. Both it and the unconscious state are sensationless, but with a vast difference between them — the difference between ignorance and knowledge. Present Yoga as an appeal to reason, as a science.

Concentration of the mind is the source of all knowledge.

Yoga teaches us to make matter our slave, as it ought to be. Yoga means "yoke", "to join", that is, to join the soul of man with the supreme Soul or God.

The mind acts in and under consciousness. What we call consciousness is only one link in the infinite chain that is our nature.

This "I" of ours covers just a little consciousness and a vast amount of unconsciousness, while over it, and mostly unknown to it, is the superconscious plane.

Through faithful practice, layer after layer of the mind opens before us, and each reveals new facts to us. We see as it were new worlds created before us, new powers are put into our hands, but we must not stop by the way or allow ourselves to be dazzled by these "beads of glass" when the mine of diamonds lies before us.

God alone is our goal. Failing to reach God, we die.

Three things are necessary to the student who wishes to succeed.

First. Give up all ideas of enjoyment in this world and the next, care only for God and Truth. We are here to know truth, not for enjoyment. Leave that to brutes who enjoy as we never can. Man is a thinking being and must struggle on until he conquers death, until he sees the light. He must not spend himself in vain talking that bears no fruit. Worship of society and popular opinion is idolatry. The soul has no sex, no country, no place, no time.

Second. Intense desire to know Truth and God. Be eager for them, long for them, as a drowning man longs for breath. Want only God, take nothing else, let not "seeming" cheat you any longer. Turn from all and seek only God.

Third. The six trainings: First — Restraining the mind from going outward. Second — Restraining the senses. Third — Turning the mind inward. Fourth — Suffering everything without murmuring. Fifth — Fastening the mind to one idea. Take the subject before you and think it out; never leave it. Do not count time. Sixth — Think constantly of your real nature. Get rid of superstition. Do not hypnotise yourself into a belief in your own inferiority. Day and night tell yourself what you really are, until you realise (actually realise) your oneness with God.

Without these disciplines, no results can be gained.

We can be conscious of the Absolute, but we can never express It. The moment we try to express It, we limit It and It ceases to be Absolute.

We have to go beyond sense limit and transcend even reason, and we have the power to do this.

[After practising the first lesson in breathing a week, the pupil reports to the teacher.]

First Lesson

This is a lesson seeking to bring out the individuality. Each individuality must be cultivated. All will meet at the centre. "Imagination is the door to inspiration and the basis of all thought." All prophets, poets, and discoverers have had great imaginative power. The explanation of nature is in us; the stone falls outside, but gravitation is in us, not outside. Those who stuff themselves, those who starve themselves, those who sleep too much, those who sleep too little, cannot become Yogis. Ignorance, fickleness, jealousy, laziness, and excessive attachment are the great enemies to success in Yoga practice. The three great requisites are:

First. Purity, physical and mental; all uncleanness, all that would draw the mind down, must be abandoned.

Second. Patience: At first there will be wonderful manifestations, but they will all cease. This is the hardest period, but hold fast; in the end the gain is sure if you have patience.

Third. Perseverance: Persevere through thick and thin, through health and sickness, never miss a day in practice.

The best time for practice is the junction of day and night, the calmest time in the tides of our bodies, the zero point between two states. If this cannot be done, practise upon rising and going to bed. Great personal cleanliness is necessary — a daily bath.

After bathing, sit down and hold the seat firm, that is, imagine that you sit as firm as a rock, that nothing can move you. Hold the head and shoulders and the hips in a straight line, keeping the spinal column free; all action is along it, and it must not be impaired.

Begin with your toes and think of each part of your body as perfect; picture it so in your mind, touching each part if you prefer to do so. Pass upward bit by bit until you reach the head, thinking of each as perfect, lacking nothing. Then think of the whole as perfect, an instrument given to you by God to enable you to attain Truth, the vessel in which you are to cross the ocean and reach the shores of eternal truth. When this has been done, take a long breath through both nostrils, throw it out again, and then hold it out as long as you comfortably can. Take four such breaths, then breathe naturally and pray for illumination.

"I meditate on the glory of that being who created this universe; may he illuminate my mind." Sit and meditate on this ten or fifteen minutes.

Tell your experiences to no one but your Guru.

Talk as little as possible.

Keep your thoughts on virtue; what we think we tend to become.

Holy meditation helps to burn out all mental impurities. All who are not Yogis are slaves; bond after bond must be broken to make us free.

All can find the reality beyond. If God is true, we must feel him as a fact, and if there is a soul, we ought to be able to see it and feel it.

The only way to find if there be a soul is to be something which is not the body.

The Yogis class our organs under two chief heads: organs of sense and organs of motion, or knowledge and action.

The internal organ or mind has four aspects. First — Manas, the cogitating or thinking faculty, which is usually almost entirely wasted, because uncontrolled; properly governed, it is a wonderful power. Second — Buddhi, the will (sometimes called the intellect). Third — Ahamkâra, the self-conscious egotism (from Aham). Fourth — Chitta, the substance in and through which all the faculties act, the floor of the mind as it were; or the sea in which the various faculties are waves.

Yoga is the science by which we stop Chitta from assuming, or becoming transformed into, several faculties. As the reflection of the moon on the sea is broken or blurred by the waves, so is the reflection of the Atman, the true Self, broken by the mental waves. Only when the sea is stilled to mirror-like calmness, can the reflection of the moon be seen, and only when the "mind-stuff", the Chitta is controlled to absolute calmness, is the Self to be recognised.

The mind is not the body, though it is matter in a finer form. It is not eternally bound by the body. This is proved as we get occasionally loosened from it. We can learn to do this at will by controlling the senses.

When we can do that fully, we shall control the universe, because our world is only what the senses bring us. Freedom is the test of the higher being. Spiritual life begins when you have loosened yourself from the control of the senses. He whose senses rule him is worldly — is a slave.

If we could entirely stop our mind-stuff from breaking into waves, it would put an end to our bodies. For millions of years we have worked so hard to manufacture these bodies that in the struggle we have forgotten our real purpose in getting them, which was to become perfect. We have grown to think that body-making is the end of our efforts. This is Mâyâ. We must break this delusion and return to our original aim and realise we are not the body, it is our servant.

Learn to take the mind out and to see that it is separate from the body. We endow the body with sensation and life and then think it is alive and real. We have worn it so long that we forget that it is not identical with us. Yoga is to help us put off our body when we please and see it as our servant, our instrument, not our ruler. Controlling the mental powers is the first great aim in Yoga practices. The second is concentrating them in full force upon any subject.

You cannot be a Yogi if you talk much.

Second Lesson

(These lessons are composed of notes of class talks given by Swami Vivekananda to an intimate audience in the house of Mrs. Sara C. Bull, a devoted American disciple, and were preserved by her and finally printed in 1913 for private circulation — *Ed.*)

This Yoga is known as the eightfold Yoga, because it is divided into eight principal parts. These are:

First — Yama. This is most important and has to govern the whole life; it has five divisions:

1st. Not injuring any being by thought, word, or deed.

2nd. Non-covetousness in thought, word, or deed.

3rd. Perfect chastity in thought, word, or deed.

4th. Perfect truthfulness in thought, word, or deed.

5th. Non-receiving of gifts.

Second — Niyama. The bodily care, bathing daily, dietary, etc.

Third — Âsana, posture. Hips, shoulders, and head must be held straight, leaving the spine free.

Fourth — Prânâyâma, restraining the breath (in order to get control of the Prâna or vital force).

Fifth — Pratyâhâra, turning the mind inward and restraining it from going outward, revolving the matter in the mind in order to understand it.

Sixth — Dhâranâ, concentration on one subject.

Seventh — Dhyâna, meditation.

Eighth — Samâdhi, illumination, the aim of all our efforts.

Yama and Niyama are for lifelong practice. As for the others, we do as the leech does, not leave one blade of grass before firmly grasping another. In other words, we have thoroughly to understand and practise one step before taking another.

The subject of this lesson is Pranayama, or controlling the Prana. In Raja-Yoga breathing enters the psychic plane and brings us to the spiritual. It is the fly-wheel of the whole bodily system. It acts first upon the lungs, the lungs act on the heart, the heart acts upon the circulation, this in turn upon the brain, and the brain upon the mind. The will can produce an outside sensation, and the outside sensation can arouse the will. Our wills are weak; we do not realise their power, we are so much bound up in matter. Most of our action is from outside in. Outside nature throws us off our balance, and we cannot (as we ought) throw nature off her balance. This is all wrong; the stronger power is really within.

The great saints and teachers were those who had conquered this world of thought within themselves and so spake with power. The story (For the story see Complete Works of Swami Vivekananda, Vol. I.) of the minister confined in a high tower, who was released through the efforts of his wife who brought him a beetle, honey, a silken thread, a cord, and a rope, illustrates the way we gain control of our mind by using first the physical regulation of the breath as the silken thread. That enables us to lay hold on one power after another until the rope of concentration delivers us from the prison of the body and we are free. Reaching freedom, we can discard the means used to bring us there.

Pranayama has three parts:
1st. Puraka — inhaling.
2nd. Kumbhaka — restraining.
3rd. Rechaka — exhaling.

There are two currents passing through the brain and circulating down the sides of the spine, crossing at the base and returning to the brain. One of these currents, called the "sun" (Pingalâ), starts from the left hemisphere of the brain, crosses at the base of the brain to the right side of the spine, and recrosses at the base of the spine, like one-half of the figure eight.

The other current, the "moon" (Idâ), reverses this action and completes this figure eight. Of course, the lower part is much longer than the upper. These currents flow day and night and make deposits of the great life forces at different points, commonly known as "plexuses"; but we are rarely conscious of them. By concentration we can learn to feel them and trace them over all parts of the body. These "sun" and "moon" currents are intimately connected with breathing, and by regulating this we get control of the body.

In the Katha Upanishad the body is described as the chariot, the mind is the reins, the intellect is the charioteer, the senses are the horses, and the objects of the senses their road. The self is the rider, seated in the chariot. Unless the rider has understanding and can make the charioteer control his horses, he can never attain the goal; but the senses, like vicious steeds, will drag him where they please and may even destroy him. These two currents are the great "check rein" in the hands of the charioteer, and he must get control of this to control the horses. We have to get the power to become moral; until we do that, we cannot control our actions. Yoga alone enables us to carry into practice the teachings of morality. To become moral is the object of Yoga. All great teachers were Yogis and controlled every current. The Yogis arrest these currents at the base of the spine and force them through the centre of the spinal column. They then become the current of knowledge, which only exists in the Yogi.

Second Lesson in Breathing: One method is not for all. This breathing must be done with rhythmic regularity, and the easiest way is by counting; as that is purely mechanical, we repeat the sacred word "Om" a certain number of times instead.

The process of Pranayama is as follows: Close the right nostril with the thumb and then slowly inhale through the left nostril, repeating the word "Om" four times.

Then firmly close both nostrils by placing the forefinger on the left one and hold the breath in, mentally repeating "Om" eight times.

Then, removing the thumb from the right nostril, exhale slowly through that, repeating "Om" four times.

As you close the exhalation, draw in the abdomen forcibly to expel all the air from the lungs. Then slowly inhale through the right nostril, keeping the left one closed, repeating "Om" four times. Next close the right nostril with the thumb and hold the breath while repeating "Om" eight times. Then unclose the left nostril and slowly exhale, repeating "Om" four times, drawing in the abdomen as before. Repeat this whole operation twice at each sitting, that is, making four Pranayamas, two for each nostril. Before taking your seat it is well to begin with prayer.

This needs to be practised a week; then gradually increase the duration of breathing, keeping the same ratio, that is, if you repeat "Om" six times at inhalation, then do the same at exhalation and twelve times during Kumbhaka. These exercises will make us more spiritual, more pure, more holy. Do not be led aside into any byways or seek after power. Love is the only power that stays by us and increases. He who seeks to come to God through Raja-Yoga must be strong mentally, physically, morally, and spiritually. Take every step in that light.

Of hundreds of thousands only one soul will say, "I will go beyond, and I will penetrate to God." Few can face the truth; but to accomplish anything, we must be willing to die for Truth.

Third Lesson

(These lessons are composed of notes of class talks given by Swami Vivekananda to an intimate audience in the house of Mrs. Sara C. Bull, a devoted American disciple, and were preserved by her and finally printed in 1913 for private circulation — *Ed.*)

Kundalini: Realise the soul not as matter, but as it is. We are thinking of the soul as body, but we must separate it from sense and thought. Then alone can we know we are immortal. Change implies the duality of cause and effect, and all that changes must be mortal. This proves that the body cannot be immortal, nor can the mind, because both are constantly changing. Only the unchangeable can be immortal, because there is nothing to act upon it.

We do not become it, we are it; but we have to clear away the veil of ignorance that hides the truth from us. The body is objectified thought. The "sun" and "moon" currents bring energy to all parts of the body. The surplus energy is stored at certain points (plexuses) along the spinal column commonly known as nerve centres.

These currents are not to be found in dead bodies and can only be traced in a healthy organism.

The Yogi has an advantage; for he is able not only to feel them, but actually to see them. They are luminous in his life, and so are the great nerve centres.

There is conscious as well as unconscious action. The Yogis possess a third kind, the superconscious, which in all countries and in all ages has been the source of all religious knowledge. The superconscious state makes no mistakes, but whereas the action of the instinct would be purely mechanical, the former is beyond consciousness.

It has been called inspiration, but the Yogi says, "This faculty is in every human being, and eventually all will enjoy it."

We must give a new direction to the "sun" and "moon" currents and open for them a new passage through the centre of the spinal cord. When we succeed in bringing the currents through this passage called "Sushumnâ", up to the brain, we are for the time being separated entirely from the body.

The nerve centre at the base of the spine near the sacrum is most important. It is the seat of the generative substance of the sexual energy and is symbolised by the Yogi as a triangle containing a tiny serpent coiled up in it. This sleeping serpent is called Kundalini, and to raise this Kundalini is the whole object of Raja-Yoga.

The great sexual force, raised from animal action and sent upward to the great dynamo of the human system, the brain, and there stored up, becomes Ojas or spiritual force. All good thought, all prayer, resolves a part of that animal energy into Ojas and helps to give us spiritual power. This Ojas is the real man and in human beings alone is it possible for this storage of Ojas to be accomplished. One in whom the whole animal sex force has been transformed into Ojas is a god. He speaks with power, and his words regenerate the world.

The Yogi pictures this serpent as being slowly lifted from stage to stage until the highest, the pineal gland, is reached. No man or woman can be really spiritual until the sexual energy, the highest power possessed by man, has been converted into Ojas.

No force can be created; it can only be directed. Therefore we must learn to control the grand powers that are already in our hands and by will power make them spiritual instead of merely animal. Thus it is clearly seen that chastity is the corner-stone of all morality and of all religion. In Raja-Yoga especially, absolute chastity in thought, word, and deed is a *sine qua non*. The same laws apply to the married and the single. If one wastes the most potent forces of one's being, one cannot become spiritual.

All history teaches us that the great seers of all ages were either monks and ascetics or those who had given up married life; only the pure in life can see God.

Just before making the Prânâyâma, endeavour to visualise the triangle. Close your eyes and picture it vividly in your imagination. See it surrounded by flames and with the serpent coiled in the middle. When you can clearly see the Kundalini, place it in imagination at the base of the spine, and when restraining the breath in Kumbhaka, throw it forcibly down on the head of the serpent to awaken it. The more powerful the imagination, the more quickly will the real result be attained and the Kundalini be awakened. Until it does, imagine it does: try to feel the currents and try to force them through the Sushumna. This hastens their action.

Fourth Lesson

(These lessons are composed of notes of class talks given by Swami Vivekananda to an intimate audience in the house of Mrs. Sara C. Bull, a devoted American disciple, and were preserved by her and finally printed in 1913 for private circulation — *Ed.*)

Before we can control the mind we must study it. We have to seize this unstable mind and drag it from its wanderings and fix it on one idea. Over and over again this must be done. By power of will we must get hold of the mind and make it stop and reflect upon the glory of God.

The easiest way to get hold of the mind is to sit quiet and let it drift where it will for a while. Hold fast to the idea, "I am the witness watching my mind drifting. The mind is not I." Then see it think as if it were a thing entirely apart from yourself. Identify yourself with God, never with matter or with the mind.

Picture the mind as a calm lake stretched before you and the thoughts that come and go as bubbles rising and breaking on its surface. Make no effort to control the thoughts, but watch them and follow them in imagination as they float away. This will gradually lessen the circles. For the mind ranges over wide circles of thought and those circles widen out into ever-increasing circles, as in a pond when we throw a stone into it. We want to reverse the process and starting with a huge circle make it narrower until at last we can fix the mind on one point and make it stay there. Hold to the idea, "I am not the mind, I see that I am thinking, I am watching my mind act", and each day the identification of yourself with thought and feeling will grow less, until at last you can entirely separate yourself from the mind and actually know it to be apart from yourself.

When this is done, the mind is your servant to control as you will. The first stage of being a Yogi is to go beyond the senses. When the mind is conquered, he has reached the highest stage.

Live alone as much as possible. The seat should be of comfortable height; put first a grass mat, then a skin (fur), next a silken cover. It is better that the seat has no back and it must stand firm.

Thoughts being pictures, we should not create them. We have to exclude all thought from the mind and make it a blank; as fast as a thought comes we have to banish it. To be able to accomplish this, we must transcend matter and go beyond our body. The whole life of man is really an effort to do this.

Each soul has its own meaning: In our nature these two things are connected.

The highest ideal we have is God. Meditate on Him. We cannot know the Knower, but we are He.

Seeing evil, we are creating it. What we are, we see outside, for the world is our mirror. This little body is a little mirror we have created, but the whole universe is our body. We must think this all the time; then we shall know that we cannot die or hurt another, because he is our own. We are birthless and deathless and we ought only to love.

"This whole universe is my body; all health, all happiness is mine, because all is in the universe." Say, "I am the universe." We finally learn that all action is from us to the mirror.

Although we appear as little waves, the whole sea is at our back, and we are one with it. No wave can exist of itself.

Imagination properly employed is our greatest friend; it goes beyond reason and is the only light that takes us everywhere.

Inspiration is from within and we have to inspire ourselves by our own higher faculties.

Fifth Lesson

(These lessons are composed of notes of class talks given by Swami Vivekananda to an intimate audience in the house of Mrs. Sara C. Bull, a devoted American disciple, and were preserved by her and finally printed in 1913 for private circulation — *Ed.*)

Pratyâhâra and Dhâranâ: Krishna says, "All who seek me by whatever means will reach me", "All must reach me." Pratyahara is a gathering toward, an attempt to get hold of the mind and focus it on the desired object. The first step is to let the mind drift; watch it; see what it thinks; be only the witness. Mind is not soul or spirit. It is only matter in a finer form, and we own it and can learn to manipulate it through the nerve energies.

The body is the objective view of what we call mind (subjective). We, the Self, are beyond both body and mind; we are "Atman", the eternal, unchangeable witness. The body is crystallised thought.

When the breath is flowing through the left nostril, it is the time for rest; when through the right, for work; and when through both, the time to meditate. When we are calm and breathing equally through both nostrils, we are in the right condition for quiet meditation. It is no use trying to concentrate at first. Control of thought will come of itself.

After sufficient practice of closing the nostrils with the thumb and forefinger, we shall be able to do it by the power of will, through thought alone.

Prânâyâma is now to be slightly changed. If the student has the name of his "Ishta" (Chosen Ideal), he should use that instead of "Om" during inhalation and exhalation, and use the word "Hum" (pronounced Hoom) during Kumbhaka.

Throw the restrained breath forcibly down on the head of the Kundalini at each repetition of the word Hum and imagine that this awakens her. Identify yourself only with God. After a while thoughts will announce their coming, and we shall learn the way they begin and be aware of what we are going to think, just as on this plane we can look out and see a person coming. This stage is reached when we have learnt to separate ourselves from our minds and see ourselves as one and thought as something apart. Do not let the thoughts grasp you; stand aside, and they will die away.

Follow these holy thoughts; go with them; and when they melt away, you will find the feet of the Omnipotent God. This is the superconscious state; when the idea melts, follow it and melt with it.

Haloes are symbols of inner light and can be seen by the Yogi. Sometimes we may see a face as if surrounded by flames and in them read the character and judge without erring. We may have our Ishta come to us as a vision, and this symbol will be the one upon which we can rest easily and fully concentrate our minds.

We can imagine through all the senses, but we do so mostly through the eyes. Even imagination is half material. In other words, we cannot think without a phantasm. But since animals appear to think, yet have no words, it is probable that there is no inseparable connection between thought and images.

Try to keep up the imagination in Yoga, being careful to keep it pure and holy. We all have our peculiarities in the way of imaginative power; follow the way most natural to you; it will be the easiest.

We are the results of all reincarnations through Karma: "One lamp lighted from another", says the Buddhist — different lamps, but the same light.

Be cheerful, be brave, bathe daily, have patience, purity, and perseverance, then you will become a Yogi in truth. Never try to hurry, and if the higher powers come, remember that they are but side-paths. Do not let them tempt you from the main road; put them aside and hold fast to your only true aim-God. Seek only the Eternal, finding which we are at rest for ever; having the all, nothing is left to strive for, and we are for ever in free and perfect existence — Existence absolute, Knowledge absolute, Bliss absolute.

Sixth Lesson

(These lessons are composed of notes of class talks given by Swami Vivekananda to an intimate audience in the house of Mrs. Sara C. Bull, a devoted American disciple, and were preserved by her and finally printed in 1913 for private circulation — *Ed.*)

Sushumnâ: It is very useful to meditate on the Sushumna. You may have a vision of it come to you, and this is the best way. Then meditate for a long time on that. It is a very fine, very brilliant thread, this living passage through the spinal cord, this way of salvation through which we have to make the Kundalini rise.

In the language of the Yogi, the Sushumna has its ends in two lotuses, the lower lotus surrounding the triangle of the Kundalini and the top one in the brain surrounding the pineal gland; between these two are four other lotuses, stages on the way:

6th. Pineal Gland.
5th. Between the Eyes.
4th. Bottom of the Throat.
3rd. Level with the Heart.
2nd. Opposite the Navel.
1st. Base of Spine.

We must awaken the Kundalini, then slowly raise it from one lotus to another till the brain is reached. Each stage corresponds to a new layer of the mind.

Women Of India

(Delivered at the Shakespeare Club House, in Pasadena, California, on January 18, 1900)

SWAMI VIVEKANANDA: "Some persons desire to ask questions about Hindu Philosophy before the lecture and to question in general about India after the lecture; but the chief difficulty is I do not know what I am to lecture on. I would be very glad to lecture on any subject, either on Hindu Philosophy or on anything concerning the race, its history, or its literature. If you, ladies and gentlemen, will suggest anything, I would be very glad."

QUESTIONER: "I would like to ask, Swami, what special principle in Hindu Philosophy you would have us Americans, who are a very practical people, adopt, and what that would do for us beyond what Christianity can do."

SWAMI VIVEKANANDA: "That is very difficult for me to decide; it rests upon you. If you find anything which you think you ought to adopt, and which will be helpful, you should take that. You see I am not a missionary, and I am not going about converting people to my idea. My principle is that all such ideas are good and great, so that some of your ideas may suit some people in India, and some of our ideas may suit some people here; so ideas must be cast abroad, all over the world."

QUESTIONER: "We would like to know the result of your philosophy; has your philosophy and religion lifted your women above our women?"

SWAMI VIVEKANANDA: "You see, that is a very invidious question: I like our women and your women too."

QUESTIONER: "Well, will you tell us about your women, their customs and education, and the position they hold in the family?"

SWAMI VIVEKANANDA: "Oh, yes, those things I would be very glad to tell you. So you want to know about Indian women tonight, and not philosophy and other things?"

THE LECTURE

I must begin by saying that you may have to bear with me a good deal, because I belong to an Order of people who never marry; so my knowledge of women in all their relations, as mother, as wife, as daughter and sister, must necessarily not be so complete as it may be with other men. And then, India, I must remember, is a vast continent, not merely a country, and is inhabited by many different races. The nations of Europe are nearer to each other, more similar to each other, than the races in India. You may get just a rough idea of it if I tell you that there are eight different languages in all India. Different languages — not dialects — each having a literature of its own. The Hindi language, alone, is spoken by 100,000,000 people; the Bengali by about 60,000,000, and so on. Then, again, the four northern Indian languages differ more from the southern Indian languages than any two European languages from each other. They are entirely different, as much different as your language differs from the Japanese, so that you will be astonished to know, when I go to southern India, unless I meet some people who can talk Sanskrit, I have to speak to them in English. Furthermore, these various races differ from each other in manners, customs, food, dress, and in their methods of thought.

Then, again, there is caste. Each caste has become, as it were, a separate racial element. If a man lives long enough in India, he will be able to tell from the features what caste a man belongs to. Then, between castes, the manners and customs are different. And all these castes are exclusive; that is to say, they would meet socially, but they would not eat or drink together, nor intermarry. In those things they remain separate. They would meet and be friends to each other, but there it would end.

Although I have more opportunity than many other men to know women in general, from my position and my occupation as a preacher, continuously travelling from one place to another and coming in contact with all grades of society — (and women, even in northern India, where they do not appear before men, in many places would break this law for religion and would come to hear us preach and talk to us) — still it would be hazardous on my part to assert that I know everything about the women of India.

So I will try to place before you the ideal. In each nation, man or woman represents an ideal consciously or unconsciously being worked out. The individual is the external expression of an ideal to be embodied. The collection of such individuals is the nation, which also represents a great ideal; towards that it is moving. And, therefore, it is rightly assumed that to understand a nation you must first understand its ideal, for each nation refuses to be judged by any other standard than its own.

All growth, progress, well-being, or degradation is but relative. It refers to a certain standard, and each man to be understood has to be referred to that standard of his perfection. You see this more markedly in nations: what one nation thinks good might not be so regarded by another nation. Cousin-marriage is quite permissible in this country. Now, in India, it is illegal; not only so, it would be classed with the most horrible incest. Widow-marriage is perfectly legitimate in this country. Among the higher castes in India it would be the greatest degradation for a woman to marry twice. So, you see, we work through such different ideas that to judge one people by the other's standard would be neither just nor practicable. Therefore we must know what the ideal is that a nation has raised before itself. When speaking of different nations, we start with a general idea that there is one code of ethics and the same kind of ideals for all races; practically, however, when we come to judge of others, we think what is good for us must be good for everybody; what we do is the right thing, what we do not do, of course in others would be outrageous. I do not mean to say this as a criticism, but just to bring the truth home. When I hear Western women denounce the confining of the feet of Chinese ladies, they never seem to think of the corsets which are doing far more injury to the race. This is just one example; for you must know that cramping the feet does not do one-millionth part of the injury to the human form that the corset has done and is doing — when every organ is displaced and the spine is curved like a serpent. When measurements are taken, you can note the curvatures. I do not mean that as a criticism but just to point out to you the situation, that as you stand aghast at women of other races, thinking that you are supreme, the very reason that they do not adopt your manners and customs shows that they also stand aghast at you.

Therefore there is some misunderstanding on both sides. There is a common platform, a common ground of understanding, a common humanity, which must be the basis of our work. We ought to find out that complete and perfect human nature which is working only in parts, here and there. It has not been given to one man to have everything in perfection. You have a part to play; I, in my humble way, another; here is one who plays a little part; there, another. The perfection is the combination of all these parts. Just as with individuals, so with races. Each race has a part to play; each race has one side of human nature to develop. And we have to take all these together; and, possibly in the distant future, some race will arise in which all these marvellous individual race perfections, attained by the different races, will come together and form a new race, the like of which the world has not yet dreamed. Beyond saying that, I have no criticism to offer about anybody. I have travelled not a little in my life; I have kept my eyes open; and the more I go about the more my mouth is closed. I have no criticism to offer.

Now, the ideal woman in India is the mother, the mother first, and the mother last. The word woman calls up to the mind of the Hindu, motherhood; and God is called Mother. As children, every day, when we are boys, we have to go early in the morning with a little cup of water and place it before the mother, and mother dips her toe into it and we drink it.

In the West, the woman is wife. The idea of womanhood is concentrated there — as the wife. To the ordinary man in India, the whole force of womanhood is concentrated in motherhood. In the Western home, the wife rules. In an Indian home, the mother rules. If a mother comes into a Western home, she has to be subordinate to the wife; to the wife belongs the home. A mother always lives in our homes: the wife must be subordinate to her. See all the difference of ideas.

Now, I only suggest comparisons; I would state facts so that we may compare the two sides. Make this comparison. If you ask, "What is an Indian woman as wife?", the Indian asks, "Where is the American woman as mother? What is she, the all-glorious, who gave me this body? What is she who kept me in her body for nine months? Where is she who would give me twenty times her life, if I had need? Where is she whose love never dies, however wicked, however vile I am? Where is she, in comparison with her, who goes to the divorce court the moment I treat her a little badly? O American woman! where is she?" I will not find her in your country. I have not found the son who thinks mother is first. When we die, even then, we do not want our wives and our children to take her place. Our mother! — we want to die with our head on her lap once more, if we die before her. Where is she? Is woman a name to be coupled with the physical body only? Ay! the Hindu mind fears all those ideals which say that the flesh must cling unto the flesh. No, no! Woman! thou shalt not be coupled with anything connected with the flesh. The name has been called holy once and for ever, for what name is there which no lust can ever approach, no carnality ever come near, than the one word mother? That is the ideal in India.

I belong to an Order very much like what you have in the Mendicant Friars of the Catholic Church; that is to say, we have to go about without very much in the way of dress and beg from door to door, live thereby, preach to people when they want it, sleep where we can get a place — that way we have to follow. And the rule is that the members of this Order have to call every woman "mother"; to every woman and little girl we have to say "mother"; that is the custom. Coming to the West, that old habit remained and I would say to ladies, "Yes, mother", and they are horrified. I could not understand why they should be horrified. Later on, I discovered the reason: because that would mean that they are old. The ideal of womanhood in India is motherhood — that marvellous, unselfish, all-suffering, ever-forgiving mother. The wife walks behind-the shadow. She must imitate the life of the mother; that is her duty. But the mother is the ideal of love; she rules the family, she possesses the family. It is the father in India who thrashes the child and spanks when there is something done by the child, and always the mother puts herself between the father and the child. You see it is just the opposite here. It has become the mother's business to spank the children in this country, and poor father comes in between. You see, ideals are different. I do not mean this as any criticism. It is all good — this what you do; but our way is what we have been taught for ages. You never hear of a mother cursing the child; she is forgiving, always forgiving. Instead of "Our Father in Heaven", we say "Mother" all the time; that idea and that word are ever associated in the Hindu mind with Infinite Love, the mother's love being the nearest approach to God's love in this mortal world of ours. "Mother, O Mother, be merciful; I am wicked! Many children have been wicked, but there never was a wicked mother" — so says the great saint Râmprasâd.

There she is — the Hindu mother. The son's wife comes in as her daughter; just as the mother's own daughter married and went out, so her son married and brought in another daughter, and she has to fall in line under the government of the queen of queens, of his mother. Even I, who never married, belonging to an Order that never marries, would be disgusted if my wife, supposing I had married, dared to displease my mother. I would be disgusted. Why? Do I not worship my mother? Why should not her daughter-in-law? Whom I worship, why not she? Who is she, then, that would try to ride over my head and govern my mother? She has to wait till her womanhood is fulfilled; and the one thing that fulfils womanhood, that is womanliness in woman, is motherhood. Wait till she becomes a mother; then she will have the same right. That, according to the Hindu mind, is the great mission of woman — to become a mother. But oh, how different! Oh, how different! My father and mother fasted and prayed, for years and years, so that I would be born. They pray for every child before it is born. Says our great law-giver, Manu, giving the definition of an Aryan, "He is the Aryan, who is born through prayer". Every child not born through prayer is illegitimate, according to the great law-giver. The child must be prayed for. Those children that come with curses, that slip into the world, just in a moment of inadvertence, because that could not be prevented — what can we expect of such progeny? Mothers of America, think of that! Think in the heart of your hearts, are you ready to be women? Not any question of race or country, or that false sentiment of national pride. Who dares to be proud in this mortal life of ours, in this world of woes and miseries? What are we before this infinite force of God? But I ask you the question tonight: Do you all pray for the children to come? Are you thankful to be mothers, or not? Do you think that you are sanctified by motherhood, or not? Ask that of your minds. If you do not, your marriage is a lie, your womanhood is false, your education is superstition, and your children, if they come without prayer, will prove a curse to humanity.

See the different ideals now coming before us. From motherhood comes tremendous responsibility. There is the basis, start from that. Well, why is mother to be worshipped so much? Because our books teach that it is the pre-natal influence that gives the impetus to the child for good or evil. Go to a hundred thousand colleges, read a million books, associate with all the learned men of the world — better off you are when born with the right stamp. You are born for good or evil. The child is a born god or a born demon; that is what the books say. Education and all these things come afterwards — are a mere bagatelle. You are what you are born. Born unhealthful, how many drug stores, swallowed wholesale, will keep you well all through your life? How many people of good, healthy lives were born of weak parents, were born of sickly, blood-poisoned parents? How many? None — none. We come with a tremendous impetus for good or evil: born demons or born gods. Education or other things are a bagatelle.

Thus say our books: direct the pre-natal influence. Why should mother be worshipped? Because she made herself pure. She underwent harsh penances sometimes to keep herself as pure as purity can be. For, mind you, no woman in India thinks of giving up her body to any man; it is her own. The English, as a reform, have introduced at present what they call "Restitution of conjugal rights", but no Indian would take advantage of it. When a man comes in physical contact with his wife, the circumstances she controls through what prayers and through what vows! For that which brings forth the child is the holiest symbol of God himself. It is the greatest prayer between man and wife, the prayer that is going to bring into the world another soul fraught with a tremendous power for good or for evil. Is it a joke? Is it a simple nervous satisfaction? Is it a brute enjoyment of the body? Says the Hindu: no, a thousand times, no!

But then, following that, there comes in another idea. The idea we started with was that the ideal is the love for the mother — herself all-suffering, all-forbearing. The worship that is accorded to the mother has its fountain-head there. She was a saint to bring me into the world; she kept her body pure, her mind pure, her food pure, her clothes pure, her imagination pure, for years, because I would be born. Because she did that, she deserves worship. And what follows? Linked with motherhood is wifehood.

You Western people are individualistic. I want to do this thing because I like it; I will elbow every one. Why? Because I like to. I want my own satisfaction, so I marry this woman. Why? Because I like her. This woman marries me. Why? Because she likes me. There it ends. She and I are the only two persons in the whole, infinite world; and I marry her and she marries me — nobody else is injured, nobody else responsible. Your Johns and your Janes may go into the forest and there they may live their lives; but when they have to live in society, their marriage means a tremendous amount of good or evil to us. Their children may be veritable demons-burning, murdering, robbing, stealing, drinking, hideous, vile.

So what is the basis of the Indian's social order? It is the caste law. I am born for the caste, I live for the caste. I do not mean myself, because, having joined an Order, we are outside. I mean those that live in civil society. Born in the caste, the whole life must be lived according to caste regulation. In other words, in the present-day language of your country, the Western man is born individualistic, while the Hindu is socialistic — entirely socialistic. Now, then, the books say: if I allow you freedom to go about and marry any woman you like, and the woman to marry any man she likes, what happens? You fall in love; the father of the woman was, perchance, a lunatic or a consumptive. The girl falls in love with the face of a man whose father was a roaring drunkard. What says the law then? The law lays down that all these marriages would be illegal. The children of drunkards, consumptives, lunatics, etc., shall not be married. The deformed, humpbacked, crazy, idiotic — no marriage for them, absolutely none, says the law.

But the Mohammedan comes from Arabia, and he has his own Arabian law; so the Arabian desert law has been forced upon us. The Englishman comes with his law; he forces it upon us, so far as he can. We are conquered. He says, "Tomorrow I will marry your sister". What can we do? Our law says, those that are born of the same family, though a hundred degrees distant, must not marry, that is illegitimate, it would deteriorate or make the race sterile. That must not be, and there it stops. So I have no voice in my marriage, nor my sister. It is the caste that determines all that. We are married sometimes when children. Why? Because the caste says: if they have to be married anyway without their consent, it is better that they are married very early, before they have developed this love: if they are allowed to grow up apart, the boy may like some other girl, and the girl some other boy, and then something evil will happen; and so, says the caste, stop it there. I do not care whether my sister is deformed, or good-looking, or bad-looking: she is my sister, and that is enough; he is my brother, and that is all I need to know. So they will love each other. You may say, "Oh! they lose a great deal of enjoyment — those exquisite emotions of a man falling in love with a woman and a woman falling in love with a man. This is a sort of tame thing, loving each other like brothers and sisters, as though they have to." So be it; but the Hindu says, "We are *socialistic*. For the sake of one man's or woman's exquisite pleasure we do not want to load misery on hundreds of others."

There they are — married. The wife comes home with her husband; that is called the second marriage. Marriage at an early age is considered the first marriage, and they grow up separately with women and with their parents. When they are grown, there is a second ceremony performed, called a second marriage. And then they live together, but under the same roof with his mother and father. When she becomes a mother, she takes her place in turn as queen of the family group.

Now comes another peculiar Indian institution. I have just told you that in the first two or three castes the widows are not allowed to marry. They cannot, even if they would. Of course, it is a hardship on many. There is no denying that not all the widows like it very much, because non-marrying entails upon them the life of a student. That is to say, a student must not eat meat or fish, nor drink wine, nor dress except in white clothes, and so on; there are many regulations. We are a nation of monks — always making penance, and we like it. Now, you see, a woman never drinks wine or eats meat. It was a hardship on us when we were students, but not on the girls. Our women would feel degraded at the idea of eating meat. Men eat meat sometimes in some castes; women never. Still, not being allowed to marry must be a hardship to many; I am sure of that.

But we must go back to the idea; they are intensely *socialistic*. In the higher castes of every country you will find the statistics show that the number of women is always much larger than the number of men. Why? Because in the higher castes, for generation after generation, the women lead an easy life. They "neither toil nor spin, yet Solomon in all his glory was not arrayed like one of them". And the poor boys, they die like flies. The girl has a cat's nine lives, they say in India. You will read in the statistics that they outnumber the boys in a very short time, except now when they are taking to work quite as hard as the boys. The number of girls in the higher castes is much larger than in the lower. Conditions are quite opposite in the lower castes. There they all work hard; women a little harder, sometimes, because they have to do the domestic work. But, mind you, I never would have thought of that, but one of your American travellers, Mark Twain, writes this about India: "In spite of all that Western critics have said of

Hindu customs, I never saw a woman harnessed to a plough with a cow or to a cart with a dog, as is done in some European countries. I saw no woman or girl at work in the fields in India. On both sides and ahead (of the railway train) brown-bodied naked men and boys are ploughing in the fields. But not a woman. In these two hours I have not seen a woman or a girl working in the fields. In India, even the lowest caste never does any hard work. They generally have an easy lot compared to the same class in other nations; and as to ploughing, they never do it. "

Now, there you are. Among the lower classes the number of men is larger than the number of women; and what would you naturally expect? A woman gets more chances of marriage, the number of men being larger.

Relative to such questions as to widows not marrying: among the first two castes, the number of women is disproportionately large, and here is a dilemma. Either you have a non-marriageable widow problem and misery, or the non-husband-getting young lady problem. To face the widow problem, or the old maid problem? There you are; either of the two. Now, go back again to the idea that the Indian mind is socialistic. It says, "Now look here! we take the widow problem as the lesser one." Why? "Because they have had their chance; they have been married. If they have lost their chance, at any rate they have had one. Sit down, be quiet, and consider these poor girls-they have not had one chance of marriage." Lord bless you! I remember once in Oxford Street, it was after ten o'clock, and all those ladies coming there, hundreds and thousands of them shopping; and some man, an American, looks around, and he says, "My Lord! how many of them will ever get husbands, I wonder!" So the Indian mind said to the widows, "Well, you have had your chance, and now we are very, very sorry that such mishaps have come to you, but we cannot help it; others are waiting."

Then religion comes into the question; the Hindu religion comes in as a comfort. For, mind you, our religion teaches that marriage is something bad, it is only for the weak. The very spiritual man or woman would not marry at all. So the religious woman says, "Well, the Lord has given me a better chance. What is the use of marrying? Thank God, worship God, what is the use of my loving man?" Of course, all of them cannot put their mind on God. Some find it simply impossible. They have to suffer; but the other poor people, they should not suffer for them. Now I leave this to your judgment; but that is their idea in India.

Next we come to woman as daughter. The great difficulty in the Indian household is the daughter. The daughter and caste combined ruin the poor Hindu, because, you see, she must marry in the same caste, and even inside the caste exactly in the same order; and so the poor man sometimes has to make himself a beggar to get his daughter married. The father of the boy demands a very high price for his son, and this poor man sometimes has to sell everything just to get a husband for his daughter. The great difficulty of the Hindu's life is the daughter. And, curiously enough, the word daughter in Sanskrit is "duhitâ". The real derivation is that, in ancient times, the daughter of the family was accustomed to milk the cows, and so the word "duhita" comes from "duh", to milk; and the word "daughter" really means a milkmaid. Later on, they found a new meaning to that word "duhita", the milkmaid — she who milks away all the milk of the family. That is the second meaning.

These are the different relations held by our Indian women. As I have told you, the mother is the greatest in position, the wife is next, and the daughter comes after them. It is a most intricate and complicated series of gradation. No foreigner can understand it, even if he lives there for years. For instance, we have three forms of the personal pronoun; they are a sort of verbs in our language. One is very respectful, one is middling, and the lowest is just like *thou* and *thee*. To children and servants the last is addressed. The middling one is used with equals. You see, these are to be applied in all the intricate relations of life. For example, to my elder sister I always throughout my life use the pronoun *âpani*, but she never does in speaking to me; she says *tumi* to me. She should not, even by mistake, say *apani* to me, because that would mean a curse. Love, the love toward those that are superior, should always be expressed in that form of language. That is the custom. Similarly I would never dare address my elder sister or elder brother, much less my mother or father, as *tu* or *tum* or *tumi*. As to calling our mother and father by name, why, we would never do that. Before I knew the customs of this country, I received such a shock when the son, in a very refined family, got up and called the mother by name! However, I got used to that. That is the custom of the country. But with us, we never pronounce the name of our parents when they are present. It is always in the third person plural, even before them.

Thus we see the most complicated mesh-work in the social life of our men and our women and in our degree of relationship. We do not speak to our wives before our elders; it is only when we are alone or when inferiors are present. If I were married, I would speak to my wife before my younger sister, my nephews or nieces; but not before my elder sister or parents. I cannot talk to my sisters about their husbands at all. The idea is, we are a monastic race. The whole social organisation has that one idea before it. Marriage is thought of as something impure, something lower. Therefore the subject of love would never be talked of. I cannot read a novel before my sister, or my brothers, or my mother, or even before others. I close the book.

Then again, eating and drinking is all in the same category. We do not eat before superiors. Our women never eat before men, except they be the children or inferiors. The wife would die rather than, as she says, "munch" before her husband. Sometimes, for instance, brothers and sisters may eat together; and if I and my sister are eating, and the husband comes to the door, my sister stops, and the poor husband flies out.

These are the customs peculiar to the country. A few of these I note in different countries also. As I never married myself, I am not perfect in all my knowledge about the wife. Mother, sisters — I know what they are; and other people's wives I saw; from that I gather what I have told you.

As to education and culture, it all depends upon the man. That is to say, where the men are highly cultured, there the women are; where the men are not, women are not. Now, from the oldest times, you know, the primary education, according to the old Hindu customs, belongs to the village system. All the land from time immemorial was nationalised, as you say — belonged to the Government. There never is any private right in land. The revenue in India comes from the land, because every man holds so much land from the Government. This land is held in common by a community, it may be five, ten, twenty, or a hundred families. They govern the whole of the land, pay a certain amount of revenue to the Government, maintain a physician, a village schoolmaster, and so on.

Those of you who have read Herbert Spencer remember what he calls the "monastery system" of education that was tried in Europe and which in some parts proved a success; that is, there is one schoolmaster, whom the village keeps. These primary schools are very rudimentary, because our methods are so simple. Each boy brings a little mat; and his paper, to begin with, is palm leaves. Palm leaves first, paper is too costly. Each boy spreads his little mat and sits upon it, brings out his inkstand and his books and begins to write. A little arithmetic, some Sanskrit grammar, a little of language and accounts — these are taught in the primary school.

> A little book on ethics, taught by an old man, we learnt by heart, and I remember one of the lessons:
> "For the good of a village, a man ought to give up his family;
> For the good of a country, he ought to give up his village;
> For the good of humanity, he may give up his country;
> For the good of the world, everything."

Such verses are there in the books. We get them by heart, and they are explained by teacher and pupil. These things we learn, both boys and girls together. Later on, the education differs. The old Sanskrit universities are mainly composed of boys. The girls very rarely go up to those universities; but there are a few exceptions.

In these modern days there is a greater impetus towards higher education on the European lines, and the trend of opinion is strong towards women getting this higher education. Of course, there are some people in India who do not want it, but those who do want it carried the day. It is a strange fact that Oxford and Cambridge are closed to women today, so are Harvard and Yale; but Calcutta University opened its doors to women more than twenty years ago. I remember that the year I graduated, several girls came out and graduated — the same standard, the same course, the same in everything as the boys; and they did very well indeed. And our religion does not prevent a woman being educated at all. In this way the girl should be educated; even thus she should be trained; and in the old books we find that the universities were equally resorted to by both girls and boys, but later the education of the whole nation was neglected. What can you expect under foreign rule? The foreign conqueror is not there to do good to us; he wants his money. I studied hard for twelve years and became a graduate of Calcutta University; now I can scarcely make $5.00 a month in my country. Would you believe it? It is actually a fact. So these educational institutions of foreigners are simply to get a lot of useful, practical slaves for a little money — to turn out a host of clerks, postmasters, telegraph operators, and so on. There it is.

As a result, education for both boys and girls is neglected, entirely neglected. There are a great many things that should be done in that land; but you must always remember, if you will kindly excuse me and permit me to use one of your own proverbs, "What is sauce for the goose is sauce for the gander." Your foreign born ladies are always crying over the hardships of the Hindu woman, and never care for the hardships of the Hindu man. They are all weeping salt tears. But who are the little girls married to? Some one, when told that they are all married to old men, asked, "And what do the young men do? What! are all the girls married to old men, only to old men?" We are born old — perhaps all the men there.

The ideal of the Indian race is freedom of the soul. This world is nothing. It is a vision, a dream. This life is one of many millions like it. The whole of this nature is Maya, is phantasm, a pest house of phantasms. That is the philosophy. Babies smile at life and think it so beautiful and good, but in a few years they will have to revert to where they began. They began life crying, and they will leave it crying. Nations in the vigour of their youth think that they can do anything and everything: "We are the gods of the earth. We are the chosen people." They think that God Almighty has given them a charter to rule over all the world, to advance His plans, to do anything they like, to turn the world upside down. They have a charter to rob, murder, kill; God has given them this, and they do that because they are only babes. So empire after empire has arisen — glorious, resplendent — now vanished away — gone, nobody knows where; it may have been stupendous in its ruin.

As a drop of water upon a lotus leaf tumbles about and falls in a moment, even so is this mortal life. Everywhere we turn are ruins. Where the forest stands today was once the mighty empire with huge cities. That is the dominant idea, the tone, the colour of the Indian mind. We know, you Western people have the youthful blood coursing through your veins. We know that nations, like men, have their day. Where is Greece? Where is Rome? Where that mighty Spaniard of the other day? Who knows through it all what becomes of India? Thus they are born, and thus they die; they rise and fall. The Hindu as a child knows of the Mogul invader whose cohorts no power on earth could stop, who has left in your language the terrible word "Tartar". The Hindu has learnt his lesson. He does not want to prattle, like the babes of today. Western people, say what you have to say. This is your day. Onward, go on, babes; have your prattle out. This is the day of the babies, to prattle. We have learnt our lesson and are quiet. You have a little wealth today, and you look down upon us. Well, this is your day. Prattle, babes, prattle — this is the Hindu's attitude.

The Lord of Lords is not to be attained by much frothy speech. The Lord of Lords is not to be attained even by the powers of the intellect. He is not gained by much power of conquest. That man who knows the secret source of things and that everything else is evanescent, unto him He, the Lord, comes; unto none else. India has learnt her lesson through ages and ages of experience. She has turned her face towards Him. She has made many mistakes; loads and loads of rubbish are heaped upon the race. Never mind; what of that? What is the clearing of rubbish, the cleaning of cities, and all that? Does that give life? Those that have fine institutions, they die. And what of institutions, those tinplate Western institutions, made in five days and broken on the sixth? One of these little handful nations cannot keep alive for two centuries together. And our institutions have stood the test of ages. Says the Hindu, "Yes, we have buried all the old nations of the earth and stand here to bury all the new races also, because our ideal is not this world, but the other. Just as your ideal is, so shall you be. If your ideal is mortal, if your ideal is of this earth, so shalt thou be. If your ideal is matter, matter shalt thou be. Behold! Our ideal is the Spirit. That alone exists, nothing else exists; and like Him, we live for ever."

My Life And Mission

(Delivered at the Shakespeare Club of Pasadena, California, on January 27, 1900)

Now, ladies and gentlemen, the subject for this morning was to have been the Vedanta Philosophy. That subject itself is interesting, but rather dry and very vast.

Meanwhile, I have been asked by your president and some of the ladies and gentlemen here to tell them something about my work and what I have been doing. It may be interesting to some here, but not so much so to me. In fact, I do not quite know how to tell it to you, for this will have been the first time in my life that I have spoken on that subject.

Now, to understand what I have been trying to do, in my small way, I will take you, in imagination, to India. We have not time to go into all the details and all the ramifications of the subject; nor is it possible for you to understand all the complexities in a foreign race in this short time. Suffice it to say, I will at least try to give you a little picture of what India is like.

It is like a gigantic building all tumbled down in ruins. At first sight, then, there is little hope. It is a nation gone and ruined. But you wait and study, then you see something beyond that. The truth is that so long as the principle, the ideal, of which the outer man is the expression, is not hurt or destroyed, the man lives, and there is hope for that man. If your coat is stolen twenty times, that is no reason why you should be destroyed. You can get a new coat. The coat is unessential. The fact that a rich man is robbed does not hurt the vitality of the man, does not mean death. The man will survive.

Standing on this principle, we look in and we see — what? India is no longer a political power; it is an enslaved race. Indians have no say, no voice in their own government; they are three hundred millions of slaves — nothing more! The average income of a man in India is two shillings a month. The common state of the vast mass of the people is starvation, so that, with the least decrease in income, millions die. A little famine means death. So there, too, when I look on that side of India, I see ruin-hopeless ruin.

But we find that the Indian race never stood for wealth. Although they acquired immense wealth, perhaps more than any other nation ever acquired, yet the nation did not stand for wealth. It was a powerful race for ages, yet we find that that nation never stood for power, never went out of the country to conquer. Quite content within their own boundaries, they never fought anybody. The Indian nation never stood for imperial glory. Wealth and power, then, were not the ideals of the race.

What then? Whether they were wrong or right — that is not the question we discuss — that nation, among all the children of men, has believed, and believed intensely, that this life is not real. The real is God; and they must cling unto that God through thick and thin. In the midst of their degradation, religion came first. The Hindu man drinks religiously, sleeps religiously, walks religiously, marries religiously, robs religiously.

Did you ever see such a country? If you want to get up a gang of robbers, the leader will have to preach some sort of religion, then formulate some bogus metaphysics, and say that this method is the clearest and quickest way to get God. Then he finds a following, otherwise not. That shows that the vitality of the race, the mission of the race is religion; and because that has not been touched, therefore that race lives.

See Rome. Rome's mission was imperial power, expansion. And so soon as that was touched, Rome fell to pieces, passed out. The mission of Greece was intellect, as soon as that was touched, why, Greece passed out. So in modern times, Spain and all these modern countries. Each nation has a mission for the world. So long as that mission is not hurt, that nation lives, despite every difficulty. But as soon as its mission is destroyed, the nation collapses.

Now, that vitality of India has not been touched yet. They have not given up that, and it is still strong — in spite of all their superstitions. Hideous superstitions are there, most revolting some of them. Never mind. The national life — current is still there — the mission of the race.

The Indian nation never will be a powerful conquering people — never. They will never be a great political power; that is not their business, that is not the note India has to play in the great harmony of nations. But what has she to play? God, and God alone. She clings unto that like grim death. Still there is hope there.

So, then, after your analysis, you come to the conclusion that all these things, all this poverty and misery, are of no consequence — the man is living still, and therefore there is hope.

Well! You see religious activities going on all through the country. I do not recall a year that has not given birth to several new sects in India. The stronger the current, the more the whirlpools and eddies. Sects are not signs of decay, they are a sign of life. Let sects multiply, till the time comes when every one of us is a sect, each individual. We need not quarrel about that.

Now, take your country. (I do not mean any criticism). Here the social laws, the political formation — everything is made to facilitate man's journey in this life. He may live very happily so long as he is on this earth. Look at your streets — how clean! Your beautiful cities! And in how many ways a man can make money! How many channels to get enjoyment in this life! But, if a man here should say, "Now look here, I shall sit down under this tree and meditate; I do not want to work", why, he would have to go to jail. See! There would be no chance for him at all. None. A man can live in this society only if he falls in line. He has to join in this rush for the enjoyment of good in this life, or he dies.

Now let us go back to India. There, if a man says, "I shall go and sit on the top of that mountain and look at the tip of my nose all the rest of my days", everybody says, "Go, and Godspeed to you!" He need not speak a word. Somebody brings him a little cloth, and he is all right. But if a man says, "Behold, I am going to enjoy a little of this life", every door is closed to him.

I say that the ideas of both countries are unjust. I see no reason why a man here should not sit down and look at the tip of his nose if he likes. Why should everybody here do just what the majority does? I see no reason.

Nor why, in India, a man should not have the goods of this life and make money. But you see how those vast millions are forced to accept the opposite point of view by tyranny. This is the tyranny of the sages. This is the tyranny of the great, tyranny of the spiritual, tyranny of the intellectual, tyranny of the wise. And the tyranny of the wise, mind you, is much more powerful than the tyranny of the ignorant. The wise, the intellectual, when they take to forcing their opinions upon others, know a hundred thousand ways to make bonds and barriers which it is not in the power of the ignorant to break.

Now, I say that this thing has got to stop. There is no use in sacrificing millions and millions of people to produce one spiritual giant. If it is possible to make a society where the spiritual giant will be produced and all the rest of the people will be happy as well, that is good; but if the millions have to be ground down, that is unjust. Better that the one great man should suffer for the salvation of the world.

In every nation you will have to work through their methods. To every man you will have to speak in his own language. Now, in England or in America, if you want to preach religion to them, you will have to work through political methods — make organisations, societies, with voting, balloting, a president, and so on, because that is the language, the method of the Western race. On the other hand, if you want to speak of politics in India, you must speak through the language of religion. You will have to tell them something like this: "The man who cleans his house every morning will acquire such and such an amount of merit, he will go to heaven, or he comes to God." Unless you put it that way, they will not listen to you. It is a question of language. The thing done is the same. But with every race, you will have to speak their language in order to reach their hearts. And that is quite just. We need not fret about that.

In the Order to which I belong we are called Sannyâsins. The word means "a man who has renounced". This is a very, very, very ancient Order. Even Buddha, who was 560 years before Christ, belonged to that Order. He was one of the reformers of his Order. That was all. So ancient! You find it mentioned away back in the Vedas, the oldest book in the world. In old India there was the regulation that every man and woman, towards the end of their lives, must get out of social life altogether and think of nothing except God and their own salvation. This was to get ready for the great event — death. So old people used to become Sannyasins in those early days. Later on, young people began to give up the world. And young people are active. They could not sit down under a tree and think all the time of their own death, so they went about preaching and starting sects, and so on. Thus, Buddha, being young, started that great reform. Had he been an old man, he would have looked at the tip of his nose and died quietly.

The Order is not a church, and the people who join the Order are not priests. There is an absolute difference between the priests and the Sannyasins. In India, priesthood, like every other business in a social life, is a hereditary profession. A priest's son will become a priest, just as a carpenter's son will be a carpenter, or a blacksmith's son a blacksmith. The priest must always be married. The Hindu does not think a man is complete unless he has a wife. An unmarried man has no right to perform religious ceremonies.

The Sannyasins do not possess property, and they do not marry. Beyond that there is no organisation. The only bond that is there is the bond between the teacher and the taught — and that is peculiar to India. The teacher is not a man who comes just to teach me, and I pay him so much, and there it ends. In India it is really like an adoption. The teacher is more than my own father, and I am truly his child, his son in every respect. I owe him obedience and reverence first, before my own father even; because, they say, the father gave me this body, but he showed me the way to salvation, he is greater than father. And we carry this love, this respect for our teacher all our lives. And that is the only organisation that exists. I adopt my disciples. Sometimes the teacher will be a young man and the disciple a very old man. But never mind, he is the son, and he calls me "Father", and I have to address him as my son, my daughter, and so on.

Now, I happened to get an old man to teach me, and he was very peculiar. He did not go much for intellectual scholarship, scarcely studied books; but when he was a boy he was seized with the tremendous idea of getting truth direct. First he tried by studying his own religion. Then he got the idea that he must get the truth of other religions; and with that idea he joïned all the sects, one after another. For the time being he did exactly what they told him to do — lived with the devotees of these different sects in turn, until interpenetrated with the particular ideal of that sect. After a few years he would go to another sect. When he had gone through with all that, he came to the conclusion that they were all good. He had no criticism to offer to any one; they are all so many paths leading to the same goal. And then he said, "That is a glorious thing, that there should be so many paths, because if there were only one path, perhaps it would suit only an individual man. The more the number of paths, the more the chance for every one of us to know the truth. If I cannot be taught in one language, I will try another, and so on". Thus his benediction was for every religion.

Now, all the ideas that I preach are only an attempt to echo his ideas. Nothing is mine originally except the wicked ones, everything I say which is false and wicked. But every word that I have ever uttered which is true and good is simply an attempt to echo his voice. Read his life by Prof. Max Muller. (Ramakrishna: His Life and Sayings, first published in London in 1896. Reprinted in 1951 by Advaita Ashrama.)

Well, there at his feet I conceived these ideas — there with some other young men. I was just a boy. I went there when I was about sixteen. Some of the other boys were still younger, some a little older — about a dozen or more. And together we conceived that this ideal had to be spread. And not only spread, but made practical. That is to say, we must show the spirituality of the Hindus, the mercifulness of the Buddhists, the activity of the Christians, the brotherhood of the Mohammedans, by our practical lives. "We shall start a universal religion now and here," we said, "we will not wait".

Our teacher was an old man who would never touch a coin with his hands. He took just the little food offered, just so many yards of cotton cloth, no more. He could never be induced to take any other gift. With all these marvellous ideas, he was strict, because that made him free. The monk in India is the friend of the prince today, dines with him; and tomorrow he is with the beggar, sleeps under a tree. He must come into contact with everyone, must always move about. As the saying is, "The rolling stone gathers no moss". The last fourteen years of my life, I have never been for three months at a time in any one place — continually rolling. So do we all.

Now, this handful of boys got hold of these ideas, and all the practical results that sprang out of these ideas. Universal religion, great sympathy for the poor, and all that are very good in theory, but one must practise.

Then came the sad day when our old teacher died. We nursed him the best we could. We had no friends. Who would listen to a few boys, with their crank notions? Nobody. At least, in India, boys are nobodies. Just think of it — a dozen boys, telling people vast, big ideas, saying they are determined to work these ideas out in life. Why, everybody laughed. From laughter it became serious; it became persecution. Why, the parents of the boys came to feel like spanking every one of us. And the more we were derided, the more determined we became.

Then came a terrible time — for me personally and for all the other boys as well. But to me came such misfortune! On the one side was my mother, my brothers. My father died at that time, and we were left poor. Oh, very poor, almost starving all the time! I was the only hope of the family, the only one who could do anything to help them. I had to stand between my two worlds. On the one hand, I would have to see my mother and brothers starve unto death; on the other, I had believed that this man's ideas were for the good of India and the world, and had to be preached and worked out. And so the fight went on in my mind for days and months. Sometimes I would pray for five or six days and nights together without stopping. Oh, the agony of those days! I was living in hell! The natural affections of my boy's heart drawing me to my family — I could not bear to see those who were the nearest and dearest to me suffering. On the other hand, nobody to sympathise with me. Who would sympathise with the imaginations of a boy — imaginations that caused so much suffering to others? Who would sympathise with me? None — except one.

That one's sympathy brought blessing and hope. She was a woman. Our teacher, this great monk, was married when he was a boy and she a mere child. When he became a young man, and all this religious zeal was upon him, she came to see him. Although they had been married for long, they had not seen very much of each other until they were grown up. Then he said to his wife, "Behold, I am your husband; you have a right to this body. But I cannot live the sex life, although I have married you. I leave it to your judgment". And she wept and said, "God speed you! The Lord bless you! Am I the woman to degrade you? If I can, I will help you. Go on in your work".

That was the woman. The husband went on and became a monk in his own way; and from a distance the wife went on helping as much as she could. And later, when the man had become a great spiritual giant, she came — really, she was the first disciple — and she spent the rest of her life taking care of the body of this man. He never knew whether he was living or dying, or anything. Sometimes, when talking, he would get so excited that if he sat on live charcoals, he did not know it. Live charcoals! Forgetting all about his body, all the time.

Well, that lady, his wife, was the only one who sympathised with the idea of those boys. But she was powerless. She was poorer than we were. Never mind! We plunged into the breach. I believed, as I was living, that these ideas were going to rationalise India and bring better days to many lands and foreign races. With that belief, came the realisation that it is better that a few persons suffer than that such ideas should die out of the world. What if a mother or two brothers die? It is a sacrifice. Let it be done. No great thing can be done without sacrifice. The heart must be plucked out and the bleeding heart placed upon the altar. Then great things are done. Is there any other way? None have found it. I appeal to each one of you, to those who have accomplished any great thing. Oh, how much it has cost! What agony! What torture! What terrible suffering is behind every deed of success in every life! You know that, all of you.

And thus we went on, that band of boys. The only thing we got from those around us was a kick and a curse — that was all. Of course, we had to beg from door to door for our food: got hips and haws — the refuse of everything — a piece of bread here and there. We got hold of a broken-down old house, with hissing cobras living underneath; and because that was the cheapest, we went into that house and lived there.

Thus we went on for some years, in the meanwhile making excursions all over India, trying to bring about the idea gradually. Ten years were spent without a ray of light! Ten more years! A thousand times despondency came; but there was one thing always to keep us hopeful — the tremendous faithfulness to each other, the tremendous love between us. I have got a hundred men and women around me; if I become the devil himself tomorrow, they will say, "Here we are still! We will never give you up!" That is a great blessing. In happiness, in misery, in famine, in pain, in the grave, in heaven, or in hell who never gives me up is my friend. Is such friendship a joke? A man may have salvation through such friendship. That brings salvation if we can love like that. If we have that faithfulness, why, there is the essence of all concentration. You need not worship any gods in the world if you have that faith, that strength, that love. And that was there with us all throughout that hard time. That was there. That made us go from the Himalayas to Cape Comorin, from the Indus to the Brahmaputra.

This band of boys began to travel about. Gradually we began to draw attention: ninety per cent was antagonism, very little of it was helpful. For we had one fault: we were boys — in poverty and with all the roughness of boys. He who has to make his own way in life is a bit rough, he has not much time to be smooth and suave and polite — "my lady and my gentleman", and all that. You have seen that in life, always. He is a rough diamond, he has not much polish, he is a jewel in an indifferent casket.

And there we were. "No compromise!" was the watchword. "This is the ideal, and this has got to be carried out. If we meet the king, though we die, we must give him a bit of our minds; if the peasant, the same". Naturally, we met with antagonism.

But, mind you, this is life's experience; if you really want the good of others, the whole universe may stand against you and cannot hurt you. It must crumble before your power of the Lord Himself in you if you are sincere and really unselfish. And those boys were that. They came as children, pure and fresh from the hands of nature. Said our Master: I want to offer at the altar of the Lord only those flowers that have not even been smelled, fruits that have not been touched with the fingers. The words of the great man sustained us all. For he saw through the future life of those boys that he collected from the streets of Calcutta, so to say. People used to laugh at him when he said, "You will see — this boy, that boy, what he becomes". His faith was unalterable: "Mother showed it to me. I may be weak, but when She says this is so — She can never make mistakes — it must be so.

"So things went on and on for ten years without any light, but with my health breaking all the time. It tells on the body in the long run: sometimes one meal at nine in the evening, another time a meal at eight in the morning, another after two days, another after three days — and always the poorest and roughest thing. Who is going to give to the beggar the good things he has? And then, they have not much in India. And most of the time walking, climbing snow peaks, sometimes ten miles of hard mountain climbing, just to get a meal. They eat unleavened bread in India, and sometimes they have it stored away for twenty or thirty days, until it is harder than bricks; and then they will give a square of that. I would have to go from house to house to collect sufficient for one meal. And then the bread was so hard, it made my mouth bleed to eat it. Literally, you can break your teeth on that bread. Then I would put it in a pot and pour over it water from the river. For months and months I existed that way – of course it was telling on the health.

Then I thought, I have tried India: it is time for me to try another country. At that time your Parliament of Religions was to be held, and someone was to be sent from India. I was just a vagabond, but I said, "If you send me, I am going. I have not much to lose, and I do not care if I lose that." It was very difficult to find the money, but after a long struggle they got together just enough to pay for my passage – and I came. Came one or two months earlier, so that I found myself drifting about in the streets here, without knowing anybody.

But finally the Parliament of Religions opened, and I met kind friends, who helped me right along. I worked a little, collected funds, started two papers, and so on. After that I went over to England and worked there. At the same time I carried on the work for India in America too.

My plan for India, as it has been developed and centralised, is this: I have told you of our lives as monks there, how we go from door to door, so that religion is brought to everybody without charge, except, perhaps, a broken piece of bread. That is why you see the lowest of the low in India holding the most exalted religious ideas. It is all through the work of these monks. But ask a man, "Who are the English?" – he does not know. He says perhaps, "They are the children of those giants they speak of in those books, are they not?" "Who governs you?" "We do not know." "What is the government?" They do not know. But they know philosophy. It is a practical want of intellectual education about life on this earth they suffer from. These millions and millions of people are ready for life beyond this world – is not that enough for them? Certainly not. They must have a better piece of bread and a better piece of rag on their bodies. The great question is: How to get that better bread and better rag for these sunken millions.

First, I must tell you, there is great hope for them, because, you see, they are the gentlest people on earth. Not that they are timid. When they want to fight, they fight like demons. The best soldiers the English have are recruited from the peasantry of India. Death is a thing of no importance to them. Their attitude is "Twenty times I have died before, and I shall die many times after this. What of that?" They never turn back. They are not given to much emotion, but they make very good fighters.

Their instinct, however, is to plough. If you rob them, murder them, tax them, do anything to them, they will be quiet and gentle, so long as you leave them free to practise their religion. They never interfere with the religion of others. "Leave us liberty to worship our gods, and take everything else!" That is their attitude. When the English touch them there, trouble starts. That was the real cause of the 1857 Mutiny — they would not bear religious repression. The great Mohammedan governments were simply blown up because they touched the Indians' religion.

But aside from that, they are very peaceful, very quiet, very gentle, and, above all, not given to vice. The absence of any strong drink, oh, it makes them infinitely superior to the mobs of any other country. You cannot compare the decency of life among the poor in India with life in the slums here. A slum means poverty, but poverty does not mean sin, indecency, and vice in India. In other countries, the opportunities are such that only the indecent and the lazy need be poor. There is no reason for poverty unless one is a fool or a blackguard — the sort who want city life and all its luxuries. They will not go into the country. They say, "We are here with all the fun, and you must give us bread". But that is not the case in India, where the poor fellows work hard from morning to sunset, and somebody else takes the bread out of their hands, and their children go hungry. Notwithstanding the millions of tons of wheat raised in India, scarcely a grain passes the mouth of a peasant. He lives upon the poorest corn, which you would not feed to your canary-birds.

Now there is no reason why they should suffer such distress — these people; oh, so pure and good! We hear so much talk about the sunken millions and the degraded women of India — but none come to our help. What do they say? They say, "You can only be helped, you can only be good by ceasing to be what you are. It is useless to help Hindus." These people do not know the history of races. There will be no more India if they change their religion and their institutions, because that is the vitality of that race. It will disappear; so, really, you will have nobody to help.

Then there is the other great point to learn: that you can never help really. What can we do for each other? You are growing in your own life, I am growing in my own. It is possible that I can give you a push in your life, knowing that, in the long run, all roads lead to Rome. It is a steady growth. No national civilisation is perfect yet. Give that civilisation a push, and it will arrive at its own goal: do not strive to change it. Take away a nation's institutions, customs, and manners, and what will be left? They hold the nation together.

But here comes the very learned foreign man, and he says, "Look here; you give up all those institutions and customs of thousands of years, and take my tomfool tinpot and be happy". This is all nonsense.

We will have to help each other, but we have to go one step farther: the first thing is to become unselfish in help. "If you do just what I tell you to do, I will help you; otherwise not." Is that help?

And so, if the Hindus want to help you spiritually, there will be no question of limitations: perfect unselfishness. I give, and there it ends. It is gone from me. My mind, my powers, my everything that I have to give, is given: given with the idea to give, and no more. I have seen many times people who have robbed half the world, and they gave $20,000 "to convert the heathen". What for? For the benefit of the heathen, or for their own souls? Just think of that.

And the Nemesis of crime is working. We men try to hoodwink our own eyes. But inside the heart, He has remained, the real Self. He never forgets. We can never delude Him. His eyes will never be hoodwinked. Whenever there is any impulse of real charity, it tells, though it be at the end of a thousand years. Obstructed, it yet wakens once more to burst like a thunderbolt. And every impulse where the motive is selfish, self-seeking — though it may be launched forth with all the newspapers blazoning, all the mobs standing and cheering — it fails to reach the mark.

I am not taking pride in this. But, mark you, I have told the story of that group of boys. Today there is not a village, not a man, not a woman in India that does not know their work and bless them. There is not a famine in the land where these boys do not plunge in and try to work and rescue as many as they can. And that strikes to the heart. The people come to know it. So help whenever you can, but mind what your motive is. If it is selfish, it will neither benefit those you help, nor yourself. If it is unselfish, it will bring blessings upon them to whom it is given, and infinite blessings upon you, sure as you are living. The Lord can never be hoodwinked. The law of Karma can never be hoodwinked.

Well then, my plans are, therefore, to reach these masses of India. Suppose you start schools all over India for the poor, still you cannot educate them. How can you? The boy of four years would better go to the plough or to work, than to your school. He cannot go to your school. It is impossible. Self-preservation is the first instinct. But if the mountain does not go to Mohammed, then Mohammed can come to the mountain. Why should not education go from door to door, say I. If a ploughman's boy cannot come to education, why not meet him at the plough, at the factory, just wherever he is? Go along with him, like his shadow. But there are these hundreds and thousands of monks, educating the people on the spiritual plane; why not let these men do the same work on the intellectual plane? Why should they not talk to the masses a little about history — about many things? The ears are the best educators. The best principles in our lives were those which we heard from our mothers through our ears. Books came much later. Book-learning is nothing. Through the ears we get the best formative principles. Then, as they get more and more interested, they may come to your books too. First, let it roll on and on — that is my idea.

Well, I must tell you that I am not a very great believer in monastic systems. They have great merits, and also great defects. There should be a perfect balance between the monastics and the householders. But monasticism has absorbed all the power in India. We represent the greatest power. The monk is greater than the prince. There is no reigning sovereign in India who dares to sit down when the "yellow cloth" is there. He gives up his seat and stands. Now, that is bad, so much power, even in the hands of good men — although these monastics have been the bulwark of the people. They stand between the priestcraft and knowledge. They are the centres of knowledge and reform. They are just what the prophets were among the Jews. The prophets were always preaching against the priests, trying to throw out superstitions. So are they in India. But all the same so much power is not good there; better methods should be worked out. But you can only work in the line of least resistance. The whole national soul there is upon monasticism. You go to India and preach any religion as a householder: the Hindu people will turn back and go out. If you have given up the world, however, they say, "He is good, he has given up the world. He is a sincere man, he wants to do what he preaches." What I mean to say is this, that it represents a tremendous power. What we can do is just to transform it, give it another form. This tremendous power in the hands of the roving Sannyasins of India has got to be transformed, and it will raise the masses up.

Now, you see, we have brought the plan down nicely on paper; but I have taken it, at the same time, from the regions of idealism. So far the plan was loose and idealistic. As years went on, it became more and more condensed and accurate; I began to see by actual working its defects, and all that.

What did I discover in its working on the material plane? First, there must be centres to educate these monks in the method of education. For instance, I send one of my men, and he goes about with a camera: he has to be taught in those things himself. In India, you will find every man is quite illiterate, and that teaching requires tremendous centres. And what does all that mean? Money. From the idealistic plane you come to everyday work. Well, I have worked hard, four years in your country, and two in England. And I am very thankful that some friends came to the rescue. One who is here today with you is amongst them. There are American friends and English friends who went over with me to India, and there has been a very rude beginning. Some English people came and joined the orders. One poor man worked hard and died in India. There are an Englishman and an Englishwoman who have retired; they have some means of their own, and they have started a centre in the Himalayas, educating the children. I have given them one of the papers I have started — a copy you will find there on the table — *The Awakened India*. And there they are instructing and working among the people. I have another centre in Calcutta. Of course, all great movements must proceed from the capital. For what is a capital? It is the heart of a nation. All the blood comes into the heart and thence it is distributed; so all the wealth, all the ideas, all the education, all spirituality will converge towards the capital and spread from it.

I am glad to tell you I have made a rude beginning. But the same work I want to do, on parallel lines, for women. And my principle is: each one helps himself. My help is from a distance. There are Indian women, English women, and I hope American women will come to take up the task. As soon as they have begun, I wash my hands of it. No man shall dictate to a woman; nor a woman to a man. Each one is independent. What bondage there may be is only that of love. Women will work out their own destinies — much better, too, than men can ever do for them. All the mischief to women has come because men undertook to shape the destiny of women. And I do not want to start with any initial mistake. One little mistake made then will go on multiplying; and if you succeed, in the long run that mistake will have assumed gigantic proportions and become hard to correct. So, if I made this mistake of employing men to work out this women's part of the work, why, women will never get rid of that — it will have become a custom. But I have got an opportunity. I told you of the lady who was my Master's wife. We have all great respect for her. She never dictates to us. So it is quite safe.

That part has to be accomplished.

Buddha's Message To The World

(Delivered in San Francisco, on March 18, 1900)

Buddhism is historically the most important religion — historically, not philosophically — because it was the most tremendous religious movement that the world ever saw, the most gigantic spiritual wave ever to burst upon human society. There is no civilisation on which its effect has not been felt in some way or other.

The followers of Buddha were most enthusiastic and very missionary in spirit. They were the first among the adherents of various religions not to remain content with the limited sphere of their Mother Church. They spread far and wide. They travelled east and west, north and south. They reached into darkest Tibet; they went into Persia, Asia Minor; they went into Russia, Poland, and many other countries of the Western world. They went into China, Korea, Japan; they went into Burma, Siam, the East Indies, and beyond. When Alexander the Great, through his military conquests, brought the Mediterranean world in contact with India, the wisdom of India at once found a channel through which to spread over vast portions of Asia and Europe. Buddhist priests went out teaching among the different nations; and as they taught, superstition and priestcraft began to vanish like mist before the sun.

To understand this movement properly you should know what conditions prevailed in India at the time Buddha came, just as to understand Christianity you have to grasp the state of Jewish society at the time of Christ. It is necessary that you have an idea of Indian society six hundred years before the birth of Christ, by which time Indian civilisation had already completed its growth.

When you study the civilisation of India, you find that it has died and revived several times; this is its peculiarity. Most races rise once and then decline for ever. There are two kinds of people; those who grow continually and those whose growth comes to an end. The peaceful nations, India and China, fall down, yet rise again; but the others, once they go down, do not come up — they die. Blessed are the peacemakers, for they shall enjoy the earth.

At the time Buddha was born, India was in need of a great spiritual leader, a prophet. There was already a most powerful body of priests. You will understand the situation better if you remember the history of the Jews — how they had two types of religious leaders, priests and prophets, the priests keeping the people in ignorance and grinding superstitions into their minds. The methods of worship the priests prescribed were only a means by which they could dominate the people. All through the Old Testament, you find the prophets challenging the superstitions of the priests. The outcome of this fight was the triumph of the prophets and the defeat of the priests.

Priests believe that there is a God, but that this God can be approached and known only through them. People can enter the Holy of Holies only with the permission of the priests. You must pay them, worship them, place everything in their hands. Throughout the history of the world, this priestly tendency has cropped up again and again — this tremendous thirst for power, this tiger-like thirst, seems a part of human nature. The priests dominate you, lay down a thousand rules for you. They describe simple truths in roundabout ways. They tell you stories to support their own superior position. If you want to thrive in this life or go to heaven after death, you have to pass through their hands. You have to perform all kinds of ceremonies and rituals. All this has made life so complicated and has so confused the brain that if I give you plain words, you will go home unsatisfied. You have become thoroughly befuddled. The less you understand, the better you feel! The prophets have been giving warnings against the priests and their superstitions and machinations; but the vast mass of people have not yet learnt to heed these warnings — education is yet to come to them.

Men must have education. They speak of democracy, of the equality of all men, these days. But how will a man know he is equal with all? He must have a strong brain, a clear mind free of nonsensical ideas; he must pierce through the mass of superstitions encrusting his mind to the pure truth that is in his inmost Self. Then he will know that all perfections, all powers are already within himself, that these have not to be given him by others. When he realises this, he becomes free that moment, he achieves equality. He also realises that every one else is equally as perfect as he, and he does not have to exercise any power, physical, mental or moral, over his brother men. He abandons the idea that there was ever any man who was lower than himself. Then he can talk of equality; not until then.

Now, as I was telling you, among the Jews there was a continuous struggle between the priests and the prophets; and the priests sought to monopolise power and knowledge, till they themselves began to lose them and the chains they had put on the feet of the people were on their own feet. The masters always become slaves before long. The culmination of the struggle was the victory of Jesus of Nazareth. This triumph is the history of Christianity. Christ at last succeeded in overthrowing the mass of witchcraft. This great prophet killed the dragon of priestly selfishness, rescued from its clutches the jewel of truth, and gave it to all the world, so that whosoever desired to possess it would have absolute freedom to do so, and would not have to wait on the pleasure of any priest or priests.

The Jews were never a very philosophical race: they had not the subtlety of the Indian brain nor did they have the Indian's psychic power. The priests in India, the Brahmins, possessed great intellectual and psychic powers. It was they who began the spiritual development of India, and they accomplished wonderful things. But the time came when the free spirit of development that had at first actuated the Brahmins disappeared. They began to arrogate powers and privileges to themselves. If a Brahmin killed a man, he would not be punished. The Brahmin, by his very birth, is the lord of the universe! Even the most wicked Brahmin must be worshipped!

But while the priests were flourishing, there existed also the poet-prophets called Sannyâsins. All Hindus, whatever their castes may be, must, for the sake of attaining spirituality, give up their work and prepare for death. No more is the world to be of any interest to them. They must go out and become Sannyasins. The Sannyasins have nothing to do with the two thousand ceremonies that the priests have invented: Pronounce certain words — ten syllables, twenty syllables, and so on — all these things are nonsense.

So these poet-prophets of ancient India repudiated the ways of the priest and declared the pure truth. They tried to break the power of the priests, and they succeeded a little. But in two generations their disciples went back to the superstitious, roundabout ways of the priests — became priests themselves: "You can get truth only through us!" Truth became crystallised again, and again prophets came to break the encrustations and free the truth, and so it went on. Yes, there must be all the time the man, the prophet, or else humanity will die.

You wonder why there have to be all these roundabout methods of the priests. Why can you not come directly to the truth? Are you ashamed of God's truth that you have to hide it behind all kinds of intricate ceremonies and formulas? Are you ashamed of God that you cannot confess His truth before the world? Do you call that being religious and spiritual? The priests are the only people fit for the truth! The masses are not fit for it! It must be diluted! Water it down a little!

Take the Sermon on the Mount and the Gitâ — they are simplicity itself. Even the streetwalker can understand them. How grand! In them you find the truth clearly and simply revealed. But no, the priests would not accept that truth can be found so directly. They speak of two thousand heavens and two thousand hells. If people follow their prescriptions, they will go to heaven! If they do not obey the rules, they will go to hell!

But the people shall learn the truth. Some are afraid that if the full truth is given to all, it will hurt them. They should not be given the unqualified truth — so they say. But the world is not much better off by compromising truth. What worse can it be than it is already? Bring truth out! If it is real, it will do good. When people protest and propose other methods, they only make apologies for witchcraft.

India was full of it in Buddha's day. There were the masses of people, and they were debarred from all knowledge. If just a word of the Vedas entered the ears of a man, terrible punishment was visited upon him. The priests had made a secret of the Vedas — the Vedas that contained the spiritual truths discovered by the ancient Hindus!

At last one man could bear it no more. He had the brain, the power, and the heart — a heart as infinite as the broad sky. He felt how the masses were being led by the priests and how the priests were glorying in their power, and he wanted to do something about it. He did not want any power over any one, and he wanted to break the mental and spiritual bonds of men. His heart was large. The heart, many around us may have, and we also want to help others. But we do not have the brain; we do not know the ways and means by which help can be given. But this man had the brain to discover the means of breaking the bondages of souls. He learnt why men suffer, and he found the way out of suffering. He was a man of accomplishment, he worked everything out; he taught one and all without distinction and made them realise the peace of enlightenment. This was the man Buddha.

You know from Arnold's poem, *The Light of Asia*, how Buddha was born a prince and how the misery of the world struck him deeply; how, although brought up and living in the lap of luxury, he could not find comfort in his personal happiness and security; how he renounced the world, leaving his princess and new-born son behind; how he wandered searching for truth from teacher to teacher; and how he at last attained to enlightenment. You know about his long mission, his disciples, his organisations. You all know these things.

Buddha was the triumph in the struggle that had been going on between the priests and the prophets in India. One thing can be said for these Indian priests — they were not and never are intolerant of religion; they never have persecuted religion. Any man was allowed to preach against them. Theirs is such a religion; they never molested any one for his religious views. But they suffered from the peculiar weaknesses of all the priests: they also sought power, they also promulgated rules and regulations and made religion unnecessarily complicated, and thereby undermined the strength of those who followed their religion.

Buddha cut through all these excrescences. He preached the most tremendous truths. He taught the very gist of the philosophy of the Vedas to one and all without distinction, he taught it to the world at large, because one of his great messages was the equality of man. Men are all equal. No concession there to anybody! Buddha was the great preacher of equality. Every man and woman has the same right to attain spirituality — that was his teaching. The difference between the priests and the other castes he abolished. Even the lowest were entitled to the highest attainments; he opened the door of Nirvâna to one and all. His teaching was bold even for India. No amount of preaching can ever shock the Indian soul, but it was hard for India to swallow Buddha's doctrine. How much harder it must be for you!

His doctrine was this: Why is there misery in our life? Because we are selfish. We desire things for ourselves — that is why there is misery. What is the way out? The giving up of the self. The self does not exist; the phenomenal world, all this that we perceive, is all that exists. There is nothing called soul underlying the cycle of life and death. There is the stream of thought, one thought following another in succession, each thought coming into existence and becoming non-existent at the same moment, that is all; there is no thinker of the thought, no soul. The body is changing all the time; so is mind, consciousness. The self therefore is a delusion. All selfishness comes of holding on to the self, to this illusory self. If we know the truth that there is no self, then we will be happy and make others happy.

This was what Buddha taught. And he did not merely talk; he was ready to give up his own life for the world. He said, "If sacrificing an animal is good, sacrificing a man is better", and he offered himself as a sacrifice. He said, "This animal sacrifice is another superstition. God and soul are the two big superstitions. God is only a superstition invented by the priests. If there is a God, as these Brahmins preach, why is there so much misery in the world? He is just like me, a slave to the law of causation. If he is not bound by the law of causation, then why does he create? Such a God is not at all satisfactory. There is the ruler in heaven that rules the universe according to his sweet will and leaves us all here to die in misery — he never has the goodness to look at us for a moment. Our whole life is continuous suffering; but this is not sufficient punishment — after death we must go to places where we have other punishments. Yet we continually perform all kinds of rites and ceremonies to please this creator of the world!"

Buddha said, "These ceremonials are all wrong. There is but one ideal in the world. Destroy all delusions; what is true will remain. As soon as the clouds are gone, the sun will shine". How to kill the self? Become perfectly unselfish, ready to give up your life even for an ant. Work not for any superstition, not to please any God, not to get any reward, but because you are seeking your own release by killing your self. Worship and prayer and all that, these are all nonsense. You all say, "I thank God" — but where does He live? You do not know, and yet you are all going crazy about God.

Hindus can give up everything except their God. To deny God is to cut off the very ground from under the feet of devotion. Devotion and God the Hindus must cling to. They can never relinquish these. And here, in the teaching of Buddha, are no God and no soul — simply work. What for? Not for the self, for the self is a delusion. We shall be ourselves when this delusion has vanished. Very few are there in the world that can rise to that height and work for work's sake.

Yet the religion of Buddha spread fast. It was because of the marvellous love which, for the first time in the history of humanity, overflowed a large heart and devoted itself to the service not only of all men but of all living things — a love which did not care for anything except to find a way of release from suffering for all beings.

Man was loving God and had forgotten all about his brother man. The man who in the name of God can give up his very life, can also turn around and kill his brother man in the name of God. That was the state of the world. They would sacrifice the son for the glory of God, would rob nations for the glory of God, would kill thousands of beings for the glory of God, would drench the earth with blood for the glory of God. This was the first time they turned to the other God — man. It is man that is to be loved. It was the first wave of intense love for all men — the first wave of true unadulterated wisdom — that, starting from India, gradually inundated country after country, north, south, east, west.

This teacher wanted to make truth shine as truth. No softening, no compromise, no pandering to the priests, the powerful, the kings. No bowing before superstitious traditions, however hoary; no respect for forms and books just because they came down from the distant past. He rejected all scriptures, all forms of religious practice. Even the very language, Sanskrit, in which religion had been traditionally taught in India, he rejected, so that his followers would not have any chance to imbibe the superstitions which were associated with it.

There is another way of looking at the truth we have been discussing: the Hindu way. We claim that Buddha's great doctrine of selflessness can be better understood if it is looked at in our way. In the Upanishads there is already the great doctrine of the Âtman and the Brahman. The Atman, Self, is the same as Brahman, the Lord. This Self is all that is; It is the only reality. Mâyâ, delusion, makes us see It as different. There is one Self, not many. That one Self shines in various forms. Man is man's brother because all men are one. A man is not only my brother, say the Vedas, he is myself. Hurting any part of the universe, I only hurt myself. I am the universe. It is a delusion that I think I am Mr. So-and-so — that is the delusion.

The more you approach your real Self, the more this delusion vanishes. The more all differences and divisions disappear, the more you realise all as the one Divinity. God exists; but He is not the man sitting upon a cloud. He is pure Spirit. Where does He reside? Nearer to you than your very self. He is the Soul. How can you perceive God as separate and different from yourself? When you think of Him as some one separate from yourself, you do not know Him. He is you yourself. That was the doctrine of the prophets of India.

It is selfishness that you think that you see Mr. So-and-so and that all the world is different from you. You believe you are different from me. You do not take any thought of me. You go home and have your dinner and sleep. If I die, you still eat, drink, and are merry. But you cannot really be happy when the rest of the world is suffering. We are all one. It is the delusion of separateness that is the root of misery. Nothing exists but the Self; there is nothing else.

Buddha's idea is that there is no God, only man himself. He repudiated the mentality which underlies the prevalent ideas of God. He found it made men weak and superstitious. If you pray to God to give you everything, who is it, then, that goes out and works? God comes to those who work hard. God helps them that help themselves. An opposite idea of God weakens our nerves, softens our muscles, makes us dependent. Everything independent is happy; everything dependent is miserable. Man has infinite power within himself, and he can realise it — he can realise himself as the one infinite Self. It can be done; but you do not believe it. You pray to God and keep your powder dry all the time.

Buddha taught the opposite. Do not let men weep. Let them have none of this praying and all that. God is not keeping shop. With every breath you are praying in God. I am talking; that is a prayer. You are listening; that is a prayer. Is there ever any movement of yours, mental or physical, in which you do not participate in the infinite Divine Energy? It is all a constant prayer. If you call only a set of words prayer, you make prayer superficial. Such prayers are not much good; they can scarcely bear any real fruit.

Is prayer a magic formula, by repeating which, even is you do not work hard, you gain miraculous results? No. All have to work hard; all have to reach the depths of that infinite Energy. Behind the poor, behind the rich, there is the same infinite Energy. It is not that one man works hard, and another by repeating a few words achieves results. This universe is a constant prayer. If you take prayer in this sense, I am with you. Words are not necessary. Better is silent prayer.

The vast majority of people do not understand the meaning of this doctrine. In India any compromise regarding the Self means that we have given power into the hands of the priests and have forgotten the great teachings of the prophets. Buddha knew this; so he brushed aside all the priestly doctrines and practices and made man stand on his own feet. It was necessary for him to go against the accustomed ways of the people; he had to bring about revolutionary changes. As a result this sacrificial religion passed away from India for ever, and was never revived.

Buddhism apparently has passed away from India; but really it has not. There was an element of danger in the teaching of Buddha — it was a reforming religion. In order to bring about the tremendous spiritual change he did, he had to give many negative teachings. But if a religion emphasises the negative side too much, it is in danger of eventual destruction. Never can a reforming sect survive if it is only reforming; the formative elements alone — the real impulse, that is, the principles — live on and on. After a reform has been brought about, it is the positive side that should be emphasised; after the building is finished the scaffolding must be taken away.

It so happened in India that as time went on, the followers of Buddha emphasised the negative aspect of his teachings too much and thereby caused the eventual downfall of their religion. The positive aspects of truth were suffocated by the forces of negation; and thus India repudiated the destructive tendencies that flourished in the name of Buddhism. That was the decree of the Indian national thought.

The negative elements of Buddhism — there is no God and no soul — died out. I can say that God is the only being that exists; it is a very positive statement. He is the one reality. When Buddha says there is no soul, I say, "Man, thou art one with the universe; thou art all things." How positive! The reformative element died out; but the formative element has lived through all time. Buddha taught kindness towards lower beings; and since then there has not been a sect in India that has not taught charity to all beings, even to animals. This kindness, this mercy, this charity — greater than any doctrine — are what Buddhism left to us.

The life of Buddha has an especial appeal. All my life I have been very fond of Buddha, but not of his doctrine. I have more veneration for that character than for any other — that boldness, that fearlessness, and that tremendous love! He was born for the good of men. Others may seek God, others may seek truth for themselves; he did not even care to know truth for himself. He sought truth because people were in misery. How to help them, that was his only concern. Throughout his life he never had a thought for himself. How can we ignorant, selfish, narrow-minded human beings ever understand the greatness of this man?

And consider his marvellous brain! No emotionalism. That giant brain never was superstitious. Believe not because an old manuscript has been produced, because it has been handed down to you from your forefathers, because your friends want you to — but think for yourself; search truth for yourself; realise it yourself. Then if you find it beneficial to one and many, give it to people. Soft-brained men, weak-minded, chicken-hearted, cannot find the truth. One has to be free, and as broad as the sky. One has to have a mind that is crystal clear; only then can truth shine in it. We are so full of superstitions! Even in your country where you think you are highly educated, how full of narrownesses and superstitions you are! Just think, with all your claims to civilisation in this country, on one occasion I was refused a chair to sit on, because I was a Hindu.

Six hundred years before the birth of Christ, at the time when Buddha lived, the people of India must have had wonderful education. Extremely free-minded they must have been. Great masses followed him. Kings gave up their thrones; queens gave up their thrones. People were able to appreciate and embrace his teaching, so revolutionary, so different from what they had been taught by the priests through the ages! But their minds have been unusually free and broad.

And consider his death. If he was great in life, he was also great in death. He ate food offered to him by a member of a race similar to your American Indians. Hindus do not touch them, because they eat everything indiscriminately. He told his disciples, "Do not eat this food, but I cannot refuse it. Go to the man and tell him he has done me one of the greatest services of my life — he has released me from the body." An old man came and sat near him — he had walked miles and miles to see the Master — and Buddha taught him. When he found a disciple weeping, he reproved him, saying, "What is this? Is this the result of all my teaching? Let there be no false bondage, no dependence on me, no false glorification of this passing personality. The Buddha is not a person; he is a realisation. Work out your own salvation."

Even when dying, he would not claim any distinction for himself. I worship him for that. What you call Buddhas and Christs are only the names of certain states of realisation. Of all the teachers of the world, he was the one who taught us most to be self-reliant, who freed us not only from the bondages of our false selves but from dependence on the invisible being or beings called God or gods. He invited every one to enter into that state of freedom which he called Nirvana. All must attain to it one day; and that attainment is the complete fulfilment of man.

Discipleship

(Delivered in San Francisco, on March 29, 1900)

My subject is "Discipleship". I do not know how you will take what I have to say. It will be rather difficult for you to accept it — the ideals of teachers and disciples in this country vary so much from those in ours. An old proverb of India comes to my mind: "There are hundreds of thousands of teachers, but it is hard to find one disciple." It seems to be true. The one important thing in the attainment of spirituality is the attitude of the pupil. When the right attitude is there, illumination comes easily.

What does the disciple need in order to receive the truth? The great sages say that to attain truth takes but the twinkling of an eye — it is just a question of knowing — the dream breaks. How long does it take? In a second the dream is gone. When the illusion vanishes, how long does it take? Just the twinkling of an eye. When I know the truth, nothing happens except that the falsehood vanishes away: I took the rope for the snake, and now I see it is the rope. It is only a question of half a second and the whole thing is done. Thou art That. Thou art the Reality. How long does it take to know this? If we are God and always have been so, not to know this is most astonishing. To know this is the only natural thing. It should not take ages to find out what we have always been and what we now are.

Yet it seems difficult to realise this self-evident truth. Ages and ages pass before we begin to catch a faint glimpse of it. God is life; God is truth. We write about this; we feel in our inmost heart that this is so, that everything else than God is nothing — here today, gone tomorrow. And yet most of us remain the same all through life. We cling to untruth, and we turn our back upon truth. We do not want to attain truth. We do not want anyone to break our dream. You see, the teachers are not wanted. Who wants to learn? But if anyone wants to realise the truth and overcome illusion, if he wants to receive the truth from a teacher, he must be a true disciple.

It is not easy to be a disciple; great preparations are necessary; many conditions have to be fulfilled. Four principal conditions are laid down by the Vedantists.

The first condition is that the student who wants to know the truth must give up all desires for gain in this world or in the life to come.

The truth is not what we see. What we see is not truth as long as any desire creeps into the mind. God is true, and the world is not true. So long as there is in the heart the least desire for the world, truth will not come. Let the world fall to ruin around my ears: I do not care. So with the next life; I do not care to go to heaven. What is heaven? Only the continuation of this earth. We would be better and the little foolish dreams we are dreaming would break sooner if there were no heaven, no continuation of this silly life on earth. By going to heaven we only prolong the miserable illusions.

What do you gain in heaven? You become gods, drink nectar, and get rheumatism. There is less misery there than on earth, but also less truth. The very rich can understand truth much less than the poorer people. "It is easier for a camel to go through the eye of a needle, than for a rich man to enter into the kingdom of God." The rich man has no time to think of anything beyond his wealth and power, his comforts and indulgences. The rich rarely become religious. Why? Because they think, if they become religious, they will have no more fun in life. In the same way, there is very little chance to become spiritual in heaven; there is too much comfort and enjoyment there — the dwellers in heaven are disinclined to give up their fun.

They say there will be no more weeping in heaven. I do not trust the man who never weeps; he has a big block of granite where the heart should be. It is evident that the heavenly people have not much sympathy. There are vast masses of them over there, and we are miserable creatures suffering in this horrible place. They could pull us all out of it; but they do not. They do not weep. There is no sorrow or misery there; therefore they do not care for anyone's misery. They drink their nectar, dances go on; beautiful wives and all that.

Going beyond these things, the disciple should say, "I do not care for anything in this life nor for all the heavens that have ever existed — I do not care to go to any of them. I do not want the sense — life in any form — this identification of myself with the body — as I feel now, 'I am this body-this huge mass of flesh.' This is what I feel I am. I refuse to believe that."

The world and the heavens, all these are bound up with the senses. You do not care for the earth if you do not have any senses. Heaven also is the world. Earth, heaven, and all that is between have but one name — earth.

Therefore the disciple, knowing the past and the present and thinking of the future, knowing what prosperity means, what happiness means, gives up all these and seeks to know the truth and truth alone. This is the first condition.

The second condition is that the disciple must be able to control the internal and the external senses and must be established in several other spiritual virtues.

The external senses are the visible organs situated in different parts of the body; the internal senses are intangible. We have the external eyes, ears, nose, and so on; and we have the corresponding internal senses. We are continually at the beck and call of both these groups of senses. Corresponding to the senses are sense-objects. If any sense-objects are near by, the senses compel us to perceive them; we have no choice or independence. There is the big nose. A little fragrance is there; I have to smell it. If there were a bad odour, I would say to myself, "Do not smell it"; but nature says, "Smell", and I smell it. Just think what we have become! We have bound ourselves. I have eyes. Anything going on, good or bad, I must see. It is the same with hearing. If anyone speaks unpleasantly to me, I must hear it. My sense of hearing compels me to do so, and how miserable I feel! Curse or praise — man has got to hear. I have seen many deaf people who do not usually hear, but anything about themselves they always hear!

All these senses, external and internal, must be under the disciple's control. By hard practice he has to arrive at the stage where he can assert his mind against the senses, against the commands of nature. He should be able to say to his mind, "You are mine; I order you, do not see or hear anything", and the mind will not see or hear anything — no form or sound will react on the mind. In that state the mind has become free of the domination of the senses, has become separated from them. No longer is it attached to the senses and the body. The external things cannot order the mind now; the mind refuses to attach itself to them. Beautiful fragrance is there. The disciple says to the mind, "Do not smell", and the mind does not perceive the fragrance. When you have arrived at that point, you are just beginning to be a disciple. That is why when everybody says, "I know the truth", I say, "If you know the truth, you must have self-control; and if you have control of yourself, show it by controlling these organs."

Next, the mind must be made to quiet down. It is rushing about. Just as I sit down to meditate, all the vilest subjects in the world come up. The whole thing is nauseating. Why should the mind think thoughts I do not want it to think? I am as it were a slave to the mind. No spiritual knowledge is possible so long as the mind is restless and out of control. The disciple has to learn to control the mind. Yes, it is the function of the mind to think. But it must not think if the disciple does not want it to; it must stop thinking when he commands it to. To qualify as a disciple, this state of the mind is very necessary.

Also, the disciple must have great power of endurance. Life seems comfortable; and you find the mind behaves well when everything is going well with you. But if something goes wrong, your mind loses its balance. That is not good. Bear all evil and misery without one murmur of hurt, without one thought of unhappiness, resistance, remedy, or retaliation. That is true endurance; and that you must acquire.

Good and evil there always are in the world. Many forget there is any evil — at least they try to forget; and when evil comes upon them, they are overwhelmed by it and feel bitter. There are others who deny that there is any evil at all and consider everything good. That also is a weakness; that also proceeds from a fear of evil. If something is evil-smelling, why sprinkle it with rose water and call it fragrant? Yes, there are good and evil in the world — God has put evil in the world. But you do not have to whitewash Him. Why there is evil is none of your business. Please have faith and keep quiet.

When my Master, Shri Ramakrishna fell ill, a Brahmin suggested to him that he apply his tremendous mental power to cure himself. He said that if my Master would only concentrate his mind on the diseased part of the body, it would heal. Shri Ramakrishna answered, "What! Bring down the mind that I've given to God to this little body!" He refused to think of body and illness. His mind was continually conscious of God; it was dedicated to Him utterly. He would not use it for any other purpose.

This craving for health, wealth, long life, and the like — the so-called good — is nothing but an illusion. To devote the mind to them in order to secure them only strengthens the delusion. We have these dreams and illusions in life, and we want to have more of them in the life to come, in heaven. More and more illusion. Resist not evil. Face it! You are higher than evil.

There is this misery in the world — it has to be suffered by someone. You cannot act without making evil for somebody. And when you seek worldly good, you only avoid an evil which must be suffered by somebody else. Everyone is trying to put it on someone else's shoulders. The disciple says, "Let the miseries of the world come to me; I shall endure them all. Let others go free."

Remember the man on the cross. He could have brought legions of angels to victory; but he did not resist. He pitied those who crucified him. He endured every humiliation and suffering. He took the burden of all upon himself: "Come unto me, all ye that labour and are heavy laden, and I will give you rest." Such is true endurance. How very high he was above this life, so high that we cannot understand it, we slaves! No sooner does a man slap me in the face than my hand hits back: bang, it goes! How can I understand the greatness and blessedness of the Glorified One? How can I see the glory of it?

But I will not drag the ideal down. I feel I am the body, resisting evil. If I get a headache, I go all over the world to have it cured; I drink two thousand bottles of medicine. How can I understand these marvellous minds? I can see the ideal, but how much of that ideal? None of this consciousness of the body, of the little self, of its pleasures and pains, its hurts and comforts, none of these can reach that atmosphere. By thinking only of the spirit and keeping the mind out of matter all the time, I can catch a glimpse of that ideal. Material thought and forms of the sense-world have no place in that ideal. Take them off and put the mind upon the spirit. Forget your life and death, your pains and pleasures, your name and fame, and realise that you are neither body nor mind but the pure spirit.

When I say "I", I mean this spirit. Close your eyes and see what picture appears when you think of your "I". Is it the picture of your body that comes, or of your mental nature? If so, you have not realised your true "I" yet. The time will come, however, when as soon as you say "I" you will see the universe, the Infinite Being. Then you will have realised your true Self and found that you are infinite. That is the truth: you are the spirit, you are not matter. There is such a thing as illusion — n it one thing is taken for another: matter is taken for spirit, this body for soul. That is the tremendous illusion. It has to go.

The next qualification is that the disciple must have faith in the Guru (teacher). In the West the teacher simply gives intellectual knowledge; that is all. The relationship with the teacher is the greatest in life. My dearest and nearest relative in life is my Guru; next, my mother; then my father. My first reverence is to the Guru. If my father says, "Do this", and my Guru says, "Do not do this", I do not do it. The Guru frees my soul. The father and mother give me this body; but the Guru gives me rebirth in the soul.

We have certain peculiar beliefs. One of these is that there are some souls, a few exceptional ones, who are already free and who will be born here for the good of the world, to help the world. They are free already; they do not care for their own salvation — they want to help others. They do not require to be taught anything. From their childhood they know everything; they may speak the highest truth even when they are babies six months old.

Upon these free souls depends the spiritual growth of mankind. They are like the first lamps from which other lamps are lighted. True, the light is in everyone, but in most men it is hidden. The great souls are shining lights from the beginning. Those who come in contact with them have as it were their own lamps lighted. By this the first lamp does not lose anything; yet it communicates its light to other lamps. A million lamps are lighted; but the first lamp goes on shining with undiminished light. The first lamp is the Guru, and the lamp that is lighted from it is the disciple. The second in turn becomes the Guru, and so on. These great ones whom you call Incarnations of God are mighty spiritual giants. They come and set in motion a tremendous spiritual current by transmitting their power to their immediate disciples and through them to generation after generation of disciples.

A bishop in the Christian Church, by the laying on of hands, claims to transmit the power which he is supposed to have received from the preceding bishops. The bishop says that Jesus Christ transmitted his power to his immediate disciples and they to others, and that that is how the Christ's power has come to him. We hold that every one of us, not bishops only, ought to have such power. There is no reason why each of you cannot be a vehicle of the mighty current of spirituality.

But first you must find a teacher, a true teacher, and you must remember that he is not just a man. You may get a teacher in the body; but the real teacher is not in the body; he is not the physical man — he is not as he appears to your eyes. It may be the teacher will come to you as a human being, and you will receive the power from him. Sometimes he will come in a dream and transmit things to the world. The power of the teacher may come to us in many ways. But for us ordinary mortals the teacher must come, and our preparation must go on till he comes.

We attend lectures and read books, argue and reason about God and soul, religion and salvation. These are not spirituality, because spirituality does not exist in books or theories or in philosophies. It is not in learning or reasoning, but in actual inner growth. Even parrots can learn things by heart and repeat them. If you become learned, what of it? Asses can carry whole libraries. So when real light will come, there will be no more of this learning from books — no book-learning. The man who cannot write even his own name can be perfectly religious, and the man with all the libraries of the world in his head may fail to be. Learning is not a condition of spiritual growth; scholarship is not a condition. The touch of the Guru, the transmittal of spiritual energy, will quicken your heart. Then will begin the growth. That is the real baptism by fire. No more stopping. You go on and go on.

Some years ago one of your Christian teachers, a friend of mine, said, "You believe in Christ?" "Yes," I answered, "but perhaps with a little more reverence." "Then why don't you be baptised?" How could I be baptised? By whom? Where is the man who can give true baptism? What is baptism? Is it sprinkling some water over you, or dipping you in water, while muttering formulas?

Baptism is the direct introduction into the life of the spirit. If you receive the real baptism, you know you are not the body but the spirit. Give me that baptism if you can. If not, you are not Christians. Even after the so-called baptism which you received, you have remained the same. What is the sense of merely saying you have been baptised in the name of the Christ? Mere talk, talk — ever disturbing the world with your foolishness! "Ever steeped in the darkness of ignorance, yet considering themselves wise and learned, the fools go round and round, staggering to and fro like the blind led by the blind." (Katha Upanishad, I.ii.5) Therefore do not say you are Christians, do not brag about baptism and things of that sort.

Of course there is true baptism — there was baptism in the beginning when the Christ came to the earth and taught. The illumined souls, the great ones that come to the earth from time to time, have the power to reveal the Supernal Vision to us. This is true baptism. You see, before the formulas and ceremonies of every religion, there exists the germ of universal truth. In course of time this truth becomes forgotten; it becomes as it were strangled by forms and ceremonies. The forms remain — we find there the casket with the spirit all gone. You have the form of baptism, but few can evoke the living spirit of baptism. The form will not suffice. If we want to gain the living knowledge of the living truth, we have to be truly initiated into it. That is the ideal.

The Guru must teach me and lead me into light, make me a link in that chain of which he himself is a link. The man in the street cannot claim to be a Guru. The Guru must be a man who has known, has actually realised the Divine truth, has perceived himself as the spirit. A mere talker cannot be the Guru. A talkative fool like me can talk much, but cannot be the Guru. A true Guru will tell the disciple, "Go and sin no more"; and no more can he sin, no more has the person the power to sin.

I have seen such men in this life. I have read the Bible and all such books; they are wonderful. But the living power you cannot find in the books. The power that can transform life in a moment can be found only in the living illumined souls, those shining lights who appear among us from time to time. They alone are fit to be Gurus. You and I are only hollow talk-talk, not teachers. We are disturbing the world more by talking, making bad vibrations. We hope and pray and struggle on, and the day will come when we shall arrive at the truth, and we shall not have to speak.

"The teacher was a boy of sixteen; he taught a man of eighty. Silence was the method of the teacher; and the doubts of the disciple vanished for ever." (Dakshinâmurti-stotram, 12 (adapted).) That is the Guru. Just think, if you find such a man, what faith and love you ought to have for that person! Why, he is God Himself, nothing less than that! That is why Christ's disciples worshipped him as God. The disciple must worship the Guru as God Himself. All a man can know is the living God, God as embodied in man, until he himself has realised God. How else would he know God?

Here is a man in America, born nineteen hundred years after Christ, who does not even belong to the same race as Christ, the Jewish race. He has not seen Jesus or his family. He says, "Jesus was God. If you do not believe it, you will go to hell". We can understand how the disciples believed it — that Christ was God; he was their Guru, and they must have believed he was God. But what has this American got to do with the man born nineteen hundred years ago? This young man tells me that I do not believe in Jesus and therefore I shall have to go to hell. What does he know of Jesus? He is fit for a lunatic asylum. This kind of belief will not do. He will have to find his Guru.

Jesus may be born again, may come to you. Then, if you worship him as God, you are all right. We must all wait till the Guru comes, and the Guru must be worshipped as God. He is God, he is nothing less than that. As you look at him, the Guru gradually melts away and what is left? The Guru picture gives place to God Himself. The Guru is the bright mask which God wears in order to come to us. As we look steadily on, gradually the mask falls off and God is revealed.

"I bow to the Guru who is the embodiment of the Bliss Divine, the personification of the highest knowledge and the giver of the greatest beatitude, who is pure, perfect, one without a second, eternal, beyond pleasure and pain, beyond all thought and all qualification, transcendental". Such is in reality the Guru. No wonder the disciple looks upon him as God Himself and trusts him, reveres him, obeys him, follows him unquestioningly. This is the relation between the Guru and the disciple.

The next condition the disciple must fulfil is to conceive an extreme desire to be free.

We are like moths plunging into the flaming fire, knowing that it will burn us, knowing that the senses only burn us, that they only enhance desire. "Desire is never satiated by enjoyment; enjoyment only increases desire as butter fed into fire increases the fire." (Bhâgavata, IX. xix.14.) Desire is increased by desire. Knowing all this, people still plunge into it all the time. Life after life they have been going after the objects of desire, suffering extremely in consequence, yet they cannot give up desire. Even religion, which should rescue them from this terrible bondage of desire, they have made a means of satisfying desire. Rarely do they ask God to free them from bondage to the body and senses, from slavery to desires. Instead, they pray to Him for health and prosperity, for long life: "O God, cure my headache, give me some money or something!"

The circle of vision has become so narrow, so degraded, so beastly, so animal! None is desiring anything beyond this body. Oh, the terrible degradation, the terrible misery of it! What little flesh, the five senses, the stomach! What is the world but a combination of stomach and sex? Look at millions of men and women — that is what they are living for. Take these away from them and they will find their life empty, meaningless, and intolerable. Such are we. And such is our mind; it is continually hankering for ways and means to satisfy the hunger of the stomach and sex. All the time this is going on. There is also endless suffering; these desires of the body bring only momentary satisfaction and endless suffering. It is like drinking a cup of which the surface layer is nectar, while underneath all is poison. But we still hanker for all these things.

What can be done? Renunciation of the senses and desires is the only way out of this misery. If you want to be spiritual, you must renounce. This is the real test. Give up the world — this nonsense of the senses. There is only one real desire: to know what is true, to be spiritual. No more materialism, no more this egoism, I must become spiritual. Strong, intense must be the desire. If a man's hands and feet were so tied that he could not move and then if a burning piece of charcoal were placed on his body, he would struggle with all his power to throw it off. When I shall have that sort of extreme desire, that restless struggle, to throw off this burning world, then the time will have come for me to glimpse the Divine Truth.

Look at me. If I lose my little pocketbook with two or three dollars in it, I go twenty times into the house to find that pocketbook. The anxiety, the worry, and the struggle! If one of you crosses me, I remember it twenty years, I cannot forgive and forget it. For the little things of the senses I can struggle like that. Who is there that struggles for God that way? "Children forget everything in their play. The young are mad after the enjoyment of the senses; they do not care for anything else. The old are brooding over their past misdeeds" (Shankara). They are thinking of their past enjoyments — old men that cannot have any enjoyment. Chewing the cud — that is the best they can do. None crave for the Lord in the same intense spirit with which they crave for the things of the senses.

They all say that God is the Truth, the only thing that really exists; that spirit alone is, not matter. Yet the things they seek of God are rarely spirit. They ask always for material things. In their prayers spirit is not separated from matter. Degradation — that is what religion has turned out to be. The whole thing is becoming sham. And the years are rolling on and nothing spiritual is being attained. But man should hunger for one thing alone, the spirit, because spirit alone exists. That is the ideal. If you cannot attain it now, say, "I cannot do it; that is the ideal, I know, but I cannot follow it yet." But that is not what you do. You degrade religion to your low level and seek matter in the name of spirit. You are all atheists. You do not believe in anything except the senses. "So-and-so said such-and-such — there may be something in it. Let us try and have the fun. Possibly some benefit will come; possibly my broken leg will get straight."

Miserable are the diseased people; they are great worshippers of the Lord, for they hope that if they pray to Him He will heal them. Not that that is altogether bad — if such prayers are honest and if they remember that that is not religion. Shri Krishna says in the Gitâ (VII.16), "Four classes of people worship Me: the distressed, the seeker of material things, the inquirer, and the knower of truth." People who are in distress approach God for relief. If they are ill, they worship Him to be healed; if they lose their wealth, they pray to Him to get it back. There are other people who ask Him for all kinds of things, because they are full of desires — name, fame, wealth, position and so on. They will say, "O Virgin Mary, I will make an offering to you if I get what I want. If you are successful in granting my prayer, I will worship God and give you a part of everything." Men not so material as that, but still with no faith in God, feel inclined to know about Him. They study philosophies, read scriptures, listen to lectures, and so on. They are the inquirers. The last class are those who worship God and know Him. All these four classes of people are good, not bad. All of them worship Him.

But we are trying to be disciples. Our sole concern is to know the highest truth. Our goal is the loftiest. We have said big words to ourselves — absolute realisation and all that. Let us measure up to the words. Let us worship the spirit in spirit, standing on spirit. Let the foundation be spirit, the middle spirit, the culmination spirit. There will be no world anywhere. Let it go and whirl into space — who cares? Stand thou in the spirit! That is the goal. We know we cannot reach it yet. Never mind. Do not despair, and do not drag the ideal down. The important thing is: how much less you think of the body, of yourself as matter — as dead, dull, insentient matter; how much more you think of yourself as shining immortal being. The more you think of yourself as shining immortal spirit, the more eager you will be to be absolutely free of matter, body, and senses. This is the intense desire to be free.

The fourth and last condition of discipleship is the discrimination of the real from the unreal. There is only one thing that is real — God. All the time the mind must be drawn to Him, dedicated to Him. God exists, nothing else exists, everything else comes and goes. Any desire for the world is illusion, because the world is unreal. More and more the mind must become conscious of God alone, until everything else appears as it really is — unreal.

These are the four conditions which one who wants to be a disciple must fulfil; without fulfilling them he will not be able to come in contact with the true Guru. And even if he is fortunate enough to find him, he will not be quickened by the power that the Guru may transmit. There cannot be any compromising of these conditions. With the fulfilment of these conditions — with all these preparations — the lotus of the disciple's heart will open, and the bee shall come. Then the disciple knows that the Guru was within the body, within himself. He opens out. He realises. He crosses the ocean of life, goes beyond. He crosses this terrible ocean: and in mercy, without a thought of gain or praise, he in his turn helps others to cross.

Is Vedanta The Future Religion?

(Delivered in San Francisco on April 8, 1900)

Those of you who have been attending my lectures for the last month or so must, by this time, be familiar with the ideas contained in the Vedanta philosophy. Vedanta is the most ancient religion of the world; but it can never be said to have become popular. Therefore the question "Is it going to be the religion of the future?" is very difficult to answer.

At the start, I may tell you that I do not know whether it will ever be the religion of the vast majority of men. Will it ever be able to take hold of one whole nation such as the United States of America? Possibly it may. However, that is the question we want to discuss this afternoon.

I shall begin by telling you what Vedanta is not, and then I shall tell you what it is. But you must remember that, with all its emphasis on impersonal principles, Vedanta is not antagonistic to anything, though it does not compromise or give up the truths which it considers fundamental.

You all know that certain things are necessary to make a religion. First of all, there is the book. The power of the book is simply marvellous! Whatever it be, the book is the centre round which human allegiance gathers. Not one religion is living today but has a book. With all its rationalism and tall talk, humanity still clings to the books. In your country every attempt to start a religion without a book has failed. In India sects rise with great success, but within a few years they die down, because there is no book behind them. So in every other country.

Study the rise and fall of the Unitarian movement. It represents the best thought of your nation. Why should it not have spread like the Methodist, Baptist, and other Christian denominations? Because there was no book. On the other hand, think of the Jews. A handful of men, driven from one country to another, still hold together, because they have a book. Think of the Parsees — only a hundred thousand in the world. About a million are all that remain of the Jains in India. And do you know that these handfuls of Parsees and Jains still keep on just because of their books? The religions that are living at the present day — every one of them has a book.

The second requisite, to make a religion, is veneration for some person. He is worshipped either as the Lord of the world or as the great Teacher. Men must worship some embodied man! They must have the Incarnation or the prophet or the great leader. You find it in every religion today. Hindus and Christians — they have Incarnations: Buddhists, Mohammedans, and Jews have prophets. But it is all about the same — all their veneration twines round some person or persons.

The third requisite seems to be that a religion, to be strong and sure of itself, must believe that it alone is the truth; otherwise it cannot influence people.

Liberalism dies because it is dry, because it cannot rouse fanaticism in the human mind, because it cannot bring out hatred for everything except itself. That is why liberalism is bound to go down again and again. It can influence only small numbers of people. The reason is not hard to see. Liberalism tries to make us unselfish. But we do not want to be unselfish — we see no immediate gain in unselfishness; we gain more by being selfish. We accept liberalism as long as we are poor, have nothing. The moment we acquire money and power, we turn very conservative. The poor man is a democrat. When he becomes rich, he becomes an aristocrat. In religion, too, human nature acts in the same way.

A prophet arises, promises all kinds of rewards to those who will follow him and eternal doom to those who will not. Thus he makes his ideas spread. All existent religions that are spreading are tremendously fanatic. The more a sect hates other sects, the greater is its success and the more people it draws into its fold. My conclusion, after travelling over a good part of the world and living with many races, and in view of the conditions prevailing in the world, is that the present state of things is going to continue, in spite of much talk of universal brotherhood.

Vedanta does not believe in any of these teachings. First, it does not believe in a book — that is the difficulty to start with. It denies the authority of any book over any other book. It denies emphatically that any one book can contain all the truths about God, soul, the ultimate reality. Those of you who have read the Upanishads remember that they say again and again, "Not by the reading of books can we realise the Self."

Second, it finds veneration for some particular person still more difficult to uphold. Those of you who are students of Vedanta — by Vedanta is always meant the Upanishads — know that this is the only religion that does not cling to any person. Not one man or woman has ever become the object of worship among the Vedantins. It cannot be. A man is no more worthy of worship than any bird, any worm. We are all brothers. The difference is only in degree. I am exactly the same as the lowest worm. You see how very little room there is in Vedanta for any man to stand ahead of us and for us to go and worship him — he dragging us on and we being saved by him. Vedanta does not give you that. No book, no man to worship, nothing.

A still greater difficulty is about God. You want to be democratic in this country. It is the democratic God that Vedanta teaches.

You have a government, but the government is impersonal. Yours is not an autocratic government, and yet it is more powerful than any monarchy in the world. Nobody seems to understand that the real power, the real life, the real strength is in the unseen, the impersonal, the nobody. As a mere person separated from others, you are nothing, but as an impersonal unit of the nation that rules itself, you are tremendous. You are all one in the government — you are a tremendous power. But where exactly is the power? Each man is the power. There is no king. I see everybody equally the same. I have not to take off my hat and bow low to anyone. Yet there is a tremendous power in each man.

Vedanta is just that. Its God is not the monarch sitting on a throne, entirely apart. There are those who like their God that way — a God to be feared and propitiated. They burn candles and crawl in the dust before Him. They want a king to rule them — they believe in a king in heaven to rule them all. The king is gone from this country at least. Where is the king of heaven now? Just where the earthly king is. In this country the king has entered every one of you. You are all kings in this country. So with the religion of Vedanta. You are all Gods. One God is not sufficient. You are all Gods, says the Vedanta.

This makes Vedanta very difficult. It does not teach the old idea of God at all. In place of that God who sat above the clouds and managed the affairs of the world without asking our permission, who created us out of nothing just because He liked it and made us undergo all this misery just because He liked it, Vedanta teaches the God that is in everyone, has become everyone and everything. His majesty the king has gone from this country; the Kingdom of Heaven went from Vedanta hundreds of years ago.

India cannot give up his majesty the king of the earth — that is why Vedanta cannot become the religion of India. There is a chance of Vedanta becoming the religion of your country because of democracy. But it can become so only if you can and do clearly understand it, if you become real men and women, not people with vague ideas and superstitions in your brains, and if you want to be truly spiritual, since Vedanta is concerned only with spirituality.

What is the idea of God in heaven? Materialism. The Vedantic idea is the infinite principle of God embodied in every one of us. God sitting up on a cloud! Think of the utter blasphemy of it! It is materialism — downright materialism. When babies think this way, it may be all right, but when grown-up men try to teach such things, it is downright disgusting — that is what it is. It is all matter, all body idea, the gross idea, the sense idea. Every bit of it is clay and nothing but clay. Is that religion? It is no more religion than is the Mumbo Jumbo "religion" of Africa. God is spirit and He should be worshipped in spirit and in truth. Does spirit live only in heaven? What is spirit? We are all spirit. Why is it we do not realise it? What makes you different from me? Body and nothing else. Forget the body, and all is spirit.

These are what Vedanta has not to give. No book. No man to be singled out from the rest of mankind — "You are worms, and we are the Lord God!" — none of that. If you are the Lord God, I also am the Lord God. So Vedanta knows no sin. There are mistakes but no sin; and in the long run everything is going to be all right. No Satan — none of this nonsense. Vedanta believes in only one sin, only one in the world, and it is this: the moment you think you are a sinner or anybody is a sinner, that is sin. From that follows every other mistake or what is usually called sin. There have been many mistakes in our lives. But we are going on. Glory be unto us that we have made mistakes! Take a long look at your past life. If your present condition is good, it has been caused by all the past mistakes as well as successes. Glory be unto success! Glory be unto mistakes! Do not look back upon what has been done. Go ahead!

You see, Vedanta proposes no sin nor sinner. No God to be afraid of. He is the one being of whom we shall never be afraid, because He is our own Self. There is only one being of whom you cannot possibly be afraid; He is that. Then is not he really the most superstitious person who has fear of God? There may be someone who is afraid of his shadow; but even he is not afraid of himself. God is man's very Self. He is that one being whom you can never possibly fear. What is all this nonsense, the fear of the Lord entering into a man, making him tremble and so on? Lord bless us that we are not all in the lunatic asylum! But if most of us are not lunatics, why should we invent such ideas as fear of God? Lord Buddha said that the whole human race is lunatic, more or less. It is perfectly true, it seems.

No book, no person, no Personal God. All these must go. Again, the senses must go. We cannot be bound to the senses. At present we are tied down — like persons dying of cold in the glaciers. They feel such a strong desire to sleep, and when their friends try to wake them, warning them of death, they say, "Let me die, I want to sleep." We all cling to the little things of the senses, even if we are ruined thereby: we forget there are much greater things.

There is a Hindu legend that the Lord was once incarnated on earth as a pig. He had a pig mate and in course of time several little pigs were born to Him. He was very happy with His family, living in the mire, squealing with joy, forgetting His divine glory and lordship. The gods became exceedingly concerned and came to the earth to beg Him to give up the pig body and return to heaven. But the Lord would have none of that; He drove them away. He said He was very happy and did not want to be disturbed. Seeing no other course, the gods destroyed the pig body of the Lord. At once He regained His divine majesty and was astonished that He could have found any joy in being a pig.

People behave in the same way. Whenever they hear of the Impersonal God, they say, "What will become of my individuality? — my individuality will go!" Next time that thought comes, remember the pig, and then think what an infinite mine of happiness you have, each one of you. How pleased you are with your present condition! But when you realise what you truly are, you will be astonished that you were unwilling to give up your sense-life. What is there in your personality? It is any better than that pig life? And this you do not want to give up! Lord bless us all!

What does Vedanta teach us? In the first place, it teaches that you need not even go out of yourself to know the truth. All the past and all the future are here in the present. No man ever saw the past. Did any one of you see the past? When you think you are knowing the past, you only imagine the past in the present moment. To see the future, you would have to bring it down to the present, which is the only reality — the rest is imagination. This present is all that is. There is only the One. All is here right now. One moment in infinite time is quite as complete and all-inclusive as every other moment. All that is and was and will be is here in the present. Let anybody try to imagine anything outside of it — he will not succeed.

What religion can paint a heaven which is not like this earth? And it is all art, only this art is being made known to us gradually. We, with five senses, look upon this world and find it gross, having colour, form, sound, and the like. Suppose I develop an electric sense — all will change. Suppose my senses grow finer — you will all appear changed. If I change, you change. If I go beyond the power of the senses, you will appear as spirit and God. Things are not what they seem.

We shall understand this by and by, and then see it: all the heavens — everything — are here, now, and they really are nothing but appearances on the Divine Presence. This Presence is much greater than all the earths and heavens. People think that this world is bad and imagine that heaven is somewhere else. This world is not bad. It is God Himself if you know it. It is a hard thing even to understand, harder than to believe. The murderer who is going to be hanged tomorrow is all God, perfect God. It is very hard to understand, surely; but it can be understood.

Therefore Vedanta formulates, not universal brotherhood, but universal oneness. I am the same as any other man, as any animal — good, bad, anything. It is one body, one mind, one soul throughout. Spirit never dies. There is no death anywhere, not even for the body. Not even the mind dies. How can even the body die? One leaf may fall — does the tree die? The universe is my body. See how it continues. All minds are mine. With all feet I walk. Through all mouths I speak. In everybody I reside.

Why can I not feel it? Because of that individuality, that piggishness. You have become bound up with this mind and can only be here, not there. What is immortality? How few reply, "It is this very existence of ours!" Most people think this is all mortal and dead — that God is not here, that they will become immortal by going to heaven. They imagine that they will see God after death. But if they do not see Him here and now, they will not see Him after death. Though they all believe in immortality, they do not know that immortality is not gained by dying and going to heaven, but by giving up this piggish individuality, by not tying ourselves down to one little body. Immortality is knowing ourselves as one with all, living in all bodies, perceiving through all minds. We are bound to feel in other bodies than this one. We are bound to feel in other bodies. What is sympathy? Is there any limit to this sympathy, this feeling in our bodies? It is quite possible that the time will come when I shall feel through the whole universe.

What is the gain? The pig body is hard to give up; we are sorry to lose the enjoyment of our one little pig body! Vedanta does not say, "Give it up": it says, "Transcend it". No need of asceticism — better would be the enjoyment of two bodies, better three, living in more bodies than one! When I can enjoy through the whole universe, the whole universe is my body.

There are many who feel horrified when they hear these teachings. They do not like to be told that they are not just little pig bodies, created by a tyrant God. I tell them, "Come up!" They say they are born in sin — they cannot come up except through someone's grace. I say, "You are Divine! They answer, "You blasphemer, how dare you speak so? How can a miserable creature be God? We are sinners!" I get very much discouraged at times, you know. Hundreds of men and women tell me, "If there is no hell, how can there be any religion?" If these people go to hell of their own will, who can prevent them?

Whatever you dream and think of, you create. If it is hell, you die and see hell. If it is evil and Satan, you get a Satan. If ghosts, you get ghosts. Whatever you think, that you become. If you have to think, think good thoughts, great thoughts. This taking for granted that you are weak little worms! By declaring we are weak, we become weak, we do not become better. Suppose we put out the light, close the windows, and call the room dark. Think of the nonsense! What good does it do me to say I am a sinner? If I am in the dark, let me light a lamp. The whole thing is gone. Yet how curious is the nature of men! Though always conscious that the universal mind is behind their life, they think more of Satan, of darkness and lies. You tell them the truth — they do not see it; they like darkness better.

This forms the one great question asked by Vedanta: Why are people so afraid? The answer is that they have made themselves helpless and dependent on others. We are so lazy, we do not want to do anything for ourselves. We want a Personal God, a saviour or a prophet to do everything for us. The very rich man never walks, always goes in the carriage; but in the course of years, he wakes up one day paralysed all over. Then he begins to feel that the way he had lived was not good after all. No man can walk for me. Every time one did, it was to my injury. If everything is done for a man by another, he will lose the use of his own limbs. Anything we do ourselves, that is the only thing we do. Anything that is done for us by another never can be ours. You cannot learn spiritual truths from my lectures. If you have learnt anything, I was only the spark that brought it out, made it flash. That is all the prophets and teachers can do. All this running after help is foolishness.

You know, there are bullock carts in India. Usually two bulls are harnessed to a cart, and sometimes a sheaf of straw is dangled at the tip of the pole, a little in front of the animals but beyond their reach. The bulls try continually to feed upon the straw, but never succeed. This is exactly how we are helped! We think we are going to get security, strength, wisdom, happiness from the outside. We always hope but never realise our hope. Never does any help come from the outside.

There is no help for man. None ever was, none is, and none will be. Why should there be? Are you not men and women? Are the lords of the earth to be helped by others? Are you not ashamed? You will be helped when you are reduced to dust. But you are spirit. Pull yourself out of difficulties by yourself! Save yourself by yourself! There is none to help you — never was. To think that there is, is sweet delusion. It comes to no good.

There came a Christian to me once and said, "You are a terrible sinner." I answered, "Yes, I am. Go on." He was a Christian missionary. That man would not give me any rest. When I see him, I fly. He said, "I have very good things for you. You are a sinner and you are going to hell." I replied, "Very good, what else?" I asked him, "Where are you going?" "I am going to heaven", he answered. I said, "I will go to hell." That day he gave me up.

Here comes a Christian man and he says, "You are all doomed; but if you believe in this doctrine, Christ will help you out." If this were true — but of course it is nothing but superstition — there would be no wickedness in the Christian countries. Let us believe in it — believing costs nothing — but why is there no result? If I ask, "Why is it that there are so many wicked people?" they say, "We have to work more." Trust in God, but keep your powder dry! Pray to God, and let God come and help you out! But it is I who struggle, pray, and worship; it is I who work out my problems — and God takes the credit. This is not good. I never do it.

Once I was invited to a dinner. The hostess asked me to say grace. I said, "I will say grace to you, madam. My grace and thanks are to you." When I work, I say grace to myself. Praise be unto me that I worked hard and acquired what I have!

All the time you work hard and bless somebody else, because you are superstitious, you are afraid. No more of these superstitions bred through thousands of years! It takes a little hard work to become spiritual. Superstitions are all materialism, because they are all based on the consciousness of body, body, body. No spirit there. Spirit has no superstitions — it is beyond the vain desires of the body.

But here and there these vain desires are being projected even into the realm of the spirit. I have attended several spiritualistic meetings. In one, the leader was a woman. She said to me, "Your mother and grandfather came to me" She said that they greeted her and talked to her. But my mother is living yet! People like to think that even after death their relatives continue to exist in the same bodies, and the spiritualists play on their superstitions. I would be very sorry to know that my dead father is still wearing his filthy body. People get consolation from this, that their fathers are all encased in matter. In another place they brought me Jesus Christ. I said, "Lord, how do you do?" It makes me feel hopeless. If that great saintly man is still wearing the body, what is to become of us poor creatures? The spiritualists did not allow me to touch any of those gentlemen. Even if these were real, I would not want them. I think, "Mother, Mother! atheists — that is what people really are! Just the desire for these five senses! Not satisfied with what they have here, they want more of the same when they die!"

What is the God of Vedanta? He is principle, not person. You and I are all Personal Gods. The absolute God of the universe, the creator, preserver, and destroyer of the universe, is impersonal principle. You and I, the cat, rat, devil, and ghost, all these are Its persons — all are Personal Gods. You want to worship Personal Gods. It is the worship of your own self. If you take my advice, you will never enter any church. Come out and go and wash off. Wash yourself again and again until you are cleansed of all the superstitions that have clung to you through the ages. Or, perhaps, you do not like to do so, since you do not wash yourself so often in this country — frequent washing is an Indian custom, not a custom of your society.

I have been asked many times, "Why do you laugh so much and make so many jokes?" I become serious sometimes — when I have stomach — ache! The Lord is all blissfulness. He is the reality behind all that exists, He is the goodness, the truth in everything. You are His incarnations. That is what is glorious. The nearer you are to Him, the less you will have occasions to cry or weep. The further we are from Him, the more will long faces come. The more we know of Him, the more misery vanishes. If one who lives in the Lord becomes miserable, what is the use of living in Him? What is the use of such a God? Throw Him overboard into the Pacific Ocean! We do not want Him!

But God is the infinite, impersonal being — ever existent, unchanging, immortal, fearless; and you are all His incarnations, His embodiments. This is the God of Vedanta, and His heaven is everywhere. In this heaven dwell all the Personal Gods there are-you yourselves. Exit praying and laying flowers in the temples!

What do you pray for? To go to heaven, to get something, and let somebody else not have it. "Lord, I want more food! Let somebody else starve!" What an idea of God who is the reality, the infinite, ever blessed existence in which there is neither part nor flaw, who is ever free, ever pure, ever perfect! We attribute to Him all our human characteristics, functions, and limitations. He must bring us food and give us clothes. As a matter of fact we have to do all these things ourselves and nobody else ever did them for us. That is the plain truth.

But you rarely think of this. You imagine there is God of whom you are special favourites, who does things for you when you ask Him; and you do not ask of Him favours for all men, all beings, but only for yourself, your own family, your own people. When the Hindu is starving, you do not care; at that time you do not think that the God of the Christians is also the God of the Hindus. Our whole idea of God, our praying, our worshipping, all are vitiated by our ignorance, our foolish idea of ourselves as body. You may not like what I am saying. You may curse me today, but tomorrow you will bless me.

We must become thinkers. Every birth is painful. We must get out of materialism. My Mother would not let us get out of Her clutches; nevertheless we must try. This struggle is all the worship there is; all the rest is mere shadow. You are the Personal God. Just now I am worshipping you. This is the greatest prayer. Worship the whole world in that sense — by serving it. This standing on a high platform, I know, does not appear like worship. But if it is service, it is worship.

The infinite truth is never to be acquired. It is here all the time, undying and unborn. He, the Lord of the universe, is in every one. There is but one temple — the body. It is the only temple that ever existed. In this body, He resides, the Lord of souls and the King of kings. We do not see that, so we make stone images of Him and build temples over them. Vedanta has been in India always, but India is full of these temples — and not only temples, but also caves containing carved images. "The fool, dwelling on the bank of the Gangâ, digs a well for water!" Such are we! Living in the midst of God — we must go and make images. We project Him in the form of the image, while all the time He exists in the temple of our body. We are lunatics, and this is the great delusion.

Worship everything as God — every form is His temple. All else is delusion. Always look within, never without. Such is the God that Vedanta preaches, and such is His worship. Naturally there is no sect, no creed, no caste in Vedanta. How can this religion be the national religion of India?

Hundreds of castes! If one man touches another man's food, he cries out, "Lord help me, I am polluted!" When I returned to India after my visit to the West, several orthodox Hindus raised a howl against my association with the Western people and my breaking the rules of orthodoxy. They did not like me to teach the truths of the Vedas to the people of the West.

But how can there be these distinctions and differences? How can the rich man turn up his nose at the poor man, and the learned at the ignorant, if we are all spirit and all the same? Unless society changes, how can such a religion as Vedanta prevail? It will take thousands of years to have large numbers of truly rational human beings. It is very hard to show men new things, to give them great ideas. It is harder still to knock off old superstitions, very hard; they do not die easily. With all his education, even the learned man becomes frightened in the dark — the nursery tales come into his mind, and he see ghosts.

The meaning of the word "Veda", from which the word "Vedanta" comes, is knowledge. All knowledge is Veda, infinite as God is infinite. Nobody ever creates knowledge. Did you ever see knowledge created? It is only discovered — what was covered is uncovered. It is always here, because it is God Himself. Past, present, and future knowledge, all exist in all of us. We discover it, that is all. All this knowledge is God Himself. The Vedas are a great Sanskrit book. In our country we go down on our knees before the man who reads the Vedas, and we do not care for the man who is studying physics. That is superstition; it is not Vedanta at all. It is utter materialism. With God every knowledge is sacred. Knowledge is God. Infinite knowledge abides within every one in the fullest measure. You are not really ignorant, though you may appear to be so. You are incarnations of God, all of you. You are incarnations of the Almighty, Omnipresent, Divine Principle. You may laugh at me now, but the time will come when you will understand. You must. Nobody will be left behind.

What is the goal? This that I have spoken of — Vedanta — is not a new religion. So old — as old as God Himself. It is not confined to any time and place, it is everywhere. Everybody knows this truth. We are all working it out. The goal of the whole universe is that. This applies even to external nature — every atom is rushing towards that goal. And do you think that any of the infinite pure souls are left without knowledge of the supreme truth? All have it, all are going to the same goal — the discovery of the innate Divinity. The maniac, the murderer, the superstitious man, the man who is lynched in this country — all are travelling to the same goal. Only that which we do ignorantly we ought to do knowingly, and better.

The unity of all existence — you all have it already within yourselves. None was ever born without it. However you may deny it, it continually asserts itself. What is human love? It is more or less an affirmation of that unity: "I am one with thee, my wife, my child, my friend!" Only you are affirming the unity ignorantly. "None ever loved the husband for the husband's sake, but for the sake of the Self that is in the husband." The wife finds unity there. The husband sees himself in the wife — instinctively he does it, but he cannot do it knowingly, consciously.

The whole universe is one existence. There cannot be anything else. Out of diversities we are all going towards this universal existence. Families into tribes, tribes into races, races into nations, nations into humanity-how many wills going to the One! It is all knowledge, all science — the realisation of this unity.

Unity is knowledge, diversity is ignorance. This knowledge is your birthright. I have not to teach it to you. There never were different religions in the world. We are all destined to have salvation, whether we will it or not. You have to attain it in the long run and become free, because it is your nature to be free. We are already free, only we do not know it, and we do not know what we have been doing. Throughout all religious systems and ideals is the same morality; one thing only is preached: "Be unselfish, love others." One says, "Because Jehovah commanded." "Allah," shouted Mohammed. Another cries, "Jesus". If it was only the command of Jehovah, how could it come to those who never knew Jehovah? If it was Jesus alone who gave this command, how could any one who never knew Jesus get it? If only Vishnu, how could the Jews get it, who never were acquainted with that gentleman? There is another source, greater than all of them. Where is it? In the eternal temple of God, in the souls of all beings from the lowest to the highest. It is there — that infinite unselfishness, infinite sacrifice, infinite compulsion to go back to unity.

We have seemingly been divided, limited, because of our ignorance; and we have become as it were the little Mrs. so-and-so and Mr. so-and-so. But all nature is giving this delusion the lie every moment. I am not that little man or little woman cut off from all else; I am the one universal existence. The soul in its own majesty is rising up every moment and declaring its own intrinsic Divinity.

This Vedanta is everywhere, only you must become conscious of it. These masses of foolish beliefs and superstitions hinder us in our progress. If we can, let us throw them off and understand that God is spirit to be worshipped in spirit and in truth. Try to be materialists no more! Throw away all matter! The conception of God must be truly spiritual. All the different ideas of God, which are more or less materialistic, must go. As man becomes more and more spiritual, he has to throw off all these ideas and leave them behind. As a matter of fact, in every country there have always been a few who have been strong enough to throw away all matter and stand out in the shining light, worshipping the spirit by the spirit.

If Vedanta — this conscious knowledge that all is one spirit — spreads, the whole of humanity will become spiritual. But is it possible? I do not know. Not within thousands of years. The old superstitions must run out. You are all interested in how to perpetuate all your superstitions. Then there are the ideas of the family brother, the caste brother, the national brother. All these are barriers to the realisation of Vedanta. Religion has been religion to very few.

Most of those who have worked in the field of religion all over the world have really been political workers. That has been the history of human beings. They have rarely tried to live up uncompromisingly to the truth. They have always worshipped the god called society; they have been mostly concerned with upholding what the masses believe — their superstitions, their weakness. They do not try to conquer nature but to fit into nature, nothing else. God to India and preach a new creed — they will not listen to it. But if you tell them it is from the Vedas — "That is good!" they will say. Here I can preach this doctrine, and you — how many of you take me seriously? But the truth is all here, and I must tell you the truth.

There is another side to the question. Everyone says that the highest, the pure, truth cannot be realised all at once by all, that men have to be led to it gradually through worship, prayer, and other kinds of prevalent religious practices. I am not sure whether that is the right method or not. In India I work both ways.

In Calcutta, I have all these images and temples — in the name of God and the Vedas, of the Bible and Christ and Buddha. Let it be tried. But on the heights of the Himalayas I have a place where I am determined nothing shall enter except pure truth. There I want to work out this idea about which I have spoken to you today. There are an Englishman and an Englishwoman in charge of the place. The purpose is to train seekers of truth and to bring up children without fear and without superstition. They shall not hear about Christs and Buddhas and Shivas and Vishnus — none of these. They shall learn, from the start, to stand upon their own feet. They shall learn from their childhood that God is the spirit and should be worshipped in spirit and in truth. Everyone must be looked upon as spirit. That is the ideal. I do not know what success will come of it. Today I am preaching the thing I like. I wish I had been brought up entirely on that, without all the dualistic superstitions.

Sometimes I agree that there is some good in the dualistic method: it helps many who are weak. If a man wants you to show him the polar star, you first point out to him a bright star near it, then a less bright star, then a dim star, and then the polar star. This process makes it easy for him to see it. All the various practices and trainings, Bibles and Gods, are but the rudiments of religion, the kindergartens of religion.

But then I think of the other side. How long will the world have to wait to reach the truth if it follows this slow, gradual process? How long? And where is the surety that it will ever succeed to any appreciable degree? It has not so far. After all, gradual or not gradual, easy or not easy to the weak, is not the dualistic method based on falsehood? Are not all the prevalent religious practices often weakening and therefore wrong? They are based on a wrong idea, a wrong view of man. Would two wrong make one right? Would the lie become truth? Would darkness become light?

I am the servant of a man who has passed away. I am only the messenger. I want to make the experiment. The teachings of Vedanta I have told you about were never really experimented with before. Although Vedanta is the oldest philosophy in the world, it has always become mixed up with superstitions and everything else.

Christ said, "I and my father are one", and you repeat it. Yet it has not helped mankind. For nineteen hundred years men have not understood that saying. They make Christ the saviour of men. He is God and we are worms! Similarly in India. In every country, this sort of belief is the backbone of every sect. For thousands of years millions and millions all over the world have been taught to worship the Lord of the world, the Incarnations, the saviours, the prophets. They have been taught to consider themselves helpless, miserable creatures and to depend upon the mercy of some person or persons for salvation. There are no doubt many marvellous things in such beliefs. But even at their best, they are but kindergartens of religion, and they have helped but little. Men are still hypnotised into abject degradation. However, there are some strong souls who get over that illusion. The hour comes when great men shall arise and cast off these kindergartens of religion and shall make vivid and powerful the true religion, the worship of the spirit by the spirit.